Walk Exodus!

שׁמוֹת

Names

פקודי
ויקהל משׁה
כי תשׂא את ראשׁ
תצוה את בני ישׂראל
תרומה מאת כל אישׁ
משׁפטים אשׁר תשׂים לפניהם
יתרו כהן מדין חתן משׁה
בשׁלח פרעה את העם ולא נחם אלהים
בא אל פרעה כי אני הכבדתי את לבו
וארא אל אברהם אל יצחק ואל יעקב באל שׁדי
שׁמות בני ישׂראל הבאים מצרימה את יעקב

Jeffrey Enoch Feinberg, Ph.D.
illustrations by Kim Alan Moudy

LEDERER

Messianic Jewish Publishers
a division of
Lederer/Messianic Jewish Communications
Baltimore, Maryland

04 03 02 01 00 99   6 5 4 3 2 1

ISBN 1-880226-87-1
Library of Congress Catalog Card Number: 99-80210

Walk Exodus! belongs to
the UMJC Special Collection
of recommended resources.

Messianic Jewish Publishers
a division of
Lederer/Messianic Jewish Communications
6204 Park Heights Avenue
Baltimore, Maryland 21215
(410) 358-6471

Distributed by
Messianic Jewish Resources International
Individual order line: (800) 410-7367
Trade order line: (800) 773-MJRI (6574)
e-mail: lederer@MessianicJewish.net
www.MessianicJewish.net

Acknowledgements

Special thanks to my wife Pat,
friends Dan Swift, Kim Moudy, and Russ Resnik,
and also to my three kids,
Avi, Zack, and Shoshi,
who learned to chant their portions from Exodus
as I wrote this book.
JEF

Preface

Walk Exodus! shows the growth and transformation of Ya'akov's family into a priestly nation, also called God's first-born son among the nations. The nation is distinguished by its redemption from Egypt, then elevated to its divine calling at Sinai. There on the mount, God speaks and promises to visibly dwell in the heart of the nation! Moshe glows from the experience. The people follow God's direct command to give gifts, build a sanctuary, ordain a priesthood, and behold the magnificent Presence of the living God! Radiating glory, God fills the sanctuary with His Presence—a Presence that pledges to carry the experience of Sinai, first to the Land of Promise and later to every nation on the face of the earth!

Portion by portion, the story line unfolds. *Walk Exodus!* follows the reading cycle, week by week. Each parashah (*portion*) is sub-divided into seven segments. At a traditional bar mitzvah ceremony, seven readers ascend the bimah (*high place*) to read, with the bar mitzvah repeating the maftir (*concluding*) part, the last three to five verses. Each reads a selected segment, whether long or short. The segment has a logic of its own, but it also fits into the story line of the parashah and into the story line of the Torah as a whole.

Readers of *Walk Exodus!* are encouraged to read from the scripture before reading from the devotional commentary. In particular, take note of the seams, the first and last verses. In this way, the topic sentence and conclusion of each segment atune the reader to the story line. Build foundational understandings! A Torah-centered world view is invaluable for interpreting related Haftarah and B'rit Chadashah readings.

One can view Torah as God's revealed blueprint for human participation in covenant relationship with God. The Haftarah then reflects the prophets' call for us to return to God's ways. Finally, the B'rit Chadashah describes how Messiah redeems us and restores our walk down the path of blessing to everlasting life. Messiah came so you might have life and have it abundantly (John 10:10b). Begin your journey now!

JEF
Independence Day, 1999

"... *where the Spirit of* ADONAI *is, there is freedom. So all of us, with faces unveiled, see as in a mirror the glory of the Lord; and we are being changed into his very image, from one degree of glory to the next, by* ADONAI *the Spirit.*"

—*2 Corinthians 3:17b-18*

Walk Exodus!

The *Title page* begins with a "doodle" of a scene from the portion. Embedded in the scene, cursive Hebrew letters spell out the portion name. Below comes an entertaining synopsis in rhyme. Now on to the meat of the Word! The section titles scope out the flow of the story across the Torah portion with its related Haftarah and B'rit Chadashah readings. Finally, the key idea at the bottom features one brief phrase to help the reader focus.

The *Hiker's Log* offers a cumulative summary of what has happened to date in the story, a hint at what lies ahead, a box capsulizing the summary, and a second box listing the people, places, and events to come.

For Hebrew lovers, *Compass Work* spells out the portion name letter by letter. Scripture supplies the context for this name, and the first verse is analyzed phrase by phrase. Related Words show how the root word gets used in everyday speech.

Starting with the Rishon, each segment of Torah gets featured on a page of its own. The topic verse is quoted, key ideas are emphasized, and challenging discussion questions stimulate contemplation. Please note that the footer at the bottom of each page references the entire segment under discussion. It is recommended that the reader consult the Scripture before reading the commentary for the particular segment.

The name *Meanderings* suggests how our journey through Torah now turns to related "excursion side-trips" in the Haftarah (*Prophets*) and B'rit Chadashah (*New Covenant/New Testament*). The format matches that of the Torah sub-sections. Like the maftir, these pages feature a quote from the end of the passage being studied. Due to the brevity of this section, the

Features

reading can become quite demanding. For readers desiring to meditate on these passages, a number of cross-references (cf.) are provided. (***Please note:*** *Selections from the B'rit Chadashah are preliminary efforts to complement the annual reading cycle for the Torah and Haftarah. It is not suggested that the current selections are the only readings or the best readings for a given portion. Readers are invited to suggest alternative selections for future editions.*)

The ***Oasis*** features *Talk Your Walk*, a conclusion drawn from the portion and *Walk Your Talk*, a personal application. Remarks in ***Journey's End*** sum up all of Exodus.

Hebrew names for Torah portions, people, places, and terms of interest are sprinkled throughout the text to add cultural context to the story. The English version and/or meaning generally follows in parentheses; otherwise, check the ***Glossary***. Whenever verse numbers vary, the references for the Tanakh are given in parentheses with the Hebrew תנ״ך to identify them.

To use this volume as a daily devotional, the following reading plan is suggested:

Sunday	*Hiker's Log* and *Compass Work* (overview)
Monday	*Rishon* and *Sheni* Sections of the Torah portion
Tuesday	*Shlishi* and *R'vi'i* Sections
Wednesday	*Chamishi* and *Shishi* Sections
Thursday	*Shvi'i* and *Maftir* Sections
Friday	*Meanderings* (Haftarah and B'rit Chadashah)
Saturday	*Oasis* (summary and application)

Readers with less time might read cross-sectionally, focusing on *Hiker's Log* and *Oasis*—or studying only certain sections each cycle and saving *Meanderings* until foundations are firm.

Table of

Contents

שמות lists the sons
of Israel's names,
the tribal chiefs
along with their dames.
In Goshen they grazed
a land Yosef claims,
to keep shepherds free
from Egyptian blames.

Israel multiplied
to two million-nine.
"I AM" gave Moshe
a staff divine
to lead us out
with a mighty sign.
But Pharaoh replied,
"The might is mine!"

Walk SH'MOT!
1:1-6:1

שְׁמוֹת
Names

TORAH—Exodus 1:1-6:1
- 1st A Nation from 70 Names—Exodus 1:1
- 2nd Moshe Rescued!—Exodus 1:18
- 3rd Wake-Up Call—Exodus 2:11
- 4th The Shepherd Sees—Exodus 3:1
- 5th Lead the Leaders!—Exodus 3:16
- 6th Father-in-Law's Blessing—Exodus 4:18
- 7th Let My People Go!—Exodus 5:1
- Maftir The Mighty Hand of God—Exodus 6:1

HAFTARAH—Isaiah 27:6-28:13, 29:22-23; Jeremiah 1:1-2:3
The Power of God—Isaiah 29:23

B'RIT CHADASHAH—1 Corinthians 14:13-25
The Power of Prophecy—1 Corinthians 14:25

The Naming of a Nation

Looking Back

B'REISHEET (*in the beginning*), God commands man to be fruitful, multiply, fill the earth, and subdue it. Man disobeys. In the next generation, sibling rivalries harden. Kayin (*Cain*) kills his brother; God curses and exiles him. Later, only NOACH (*Noah/rest*) walks with God, finds chen (*favor*), and rests. He fathers three sons, builds an ark, and survives judgment.

Ten generations later, God calls to Avram, LECH L'CHA (*go forth, yourself!*). Avraham (*Abraham/father of a mass of nations*) walks with God. VAYERA יהוה (*and the LORD appeared*) to him, announcing the miraculous birth and salvation of a son from his own loins. God swears his nation will be indestructible, ekev (*as a result of*) Avraham's obedience.

B'REISHEET—in the beginning, God creates Paradise. Only NOACH rests. God calls to Avram, LECH L'CHA. VAYERA! God announces Yitzchak. CHAYEI SARAH continues through TOL'DOT. VAYETSE, VAYISHLACH, VAYESHEV— Ya'akov exits, sends gifts, and resettles as Yosef unsettles. MIKETZ—at the end, Y'hudah draws near—VAYIGASH! The family reunites, VAY'CHI—and Ya'akov lives on as the children of Yisra'el! So ends the book of Genesis. 400 years later, we are still exiled in Egypt. The story picks up as we long to make our Exodus exit. V'eleh SH'MOT—and these are the names . . .

Eternal promises of the chosen nation pass through CHAYEI SARAH (*the life of Sarah*). Rivkah succeeds Sarah, but only one of her twins inherits the eternal promises

Log

for **TOL'DOT** (*generations*) beyond. **VAYETSE** Ya'akov (*and Jacob went out*) to escape his brother's wrath and avoid inter-marriage to idolaters. He returns after twenty years. **VAYISHLACH** (*and he sent*) tribute, to repent stealing blessings of prosperity and pre-eminence.

VAYESHEV Ya'akov (*and Jacob settled*) in the Land, upon his return from exile. His family fragments, however, with Yosef now exiled. **MIKETZ** (*at the end of*) years in jail, Yosef is clothed and elevated to viceroy of Egypt. He forces famished siblings to face old rivalries.

VAYIGASH Y'hudah (*and Judah drew near*), to stop the cycle of grieving a father with jealousies of brother against brother. Ya'akov journeys to Egypt, and his family unifies! **VAY'CHI**

In SH'MOT . . .

The Key People are descendants of Ya'akov (*Jacob*), a new Par'oh (*Pharaoh*), midwives, Moshe (*Moses*), Miryam (*Miriam*), Tsiporah (*Zipporah*), Pharaoh's daughter, Yitro (*Jethro*), Gershom, and Aharon (*Aaron*).

The Scenes include Mitzrayim (*Egypt*), Midyan (*Midian*), and Chorev (*Mt. Horeb in Sinai*).

The Main Events include Ya'akov's family multiplying, enslaved in Egypt; baby Moshe hidden in basket, rescued, raised in palace, killing an Egyptian, fleeing to Midyan, and marrying; God's call from the burning bush, identified as יהוה; staff, signs, wonders, and Aharon as spokesman; first encounter with Pharaoh and tougher slavery without straw for bricks.

(*and Jacob lived*) in his son's household. V'eleh **SH'MOT** (*and these are the names*) of the sons of Yisra'el who continue Ya'akov's life as Yisra'el . . .

The Trail Ahead

The Path

וְאֵלֶּה שְׁמוֹת בְּנֵי יִשְׂרָאֵל
הַבָּאִים מִצְרַיְמָה
אֵת יַעֲקֹב
אִישׁ וּבֵיתוֹ בָּאוּ

שמות א/א—

ת	ו	מ	שׁ
letter: tav	vav	mem	shin
sound: T	**Oh**	M	SH'

names = SH'MOT = שְׁמוֹת

Work

and these (are)	*v'eleh*	וְאֵלֶּה
<u>names</u> (of)	*sh'**mot***	שְׁמוֹת
sons of Israel	*b'nei Yisra'el*	בְּנֵי יִשְׂרָאֵל
the coming ones	*ha-ba'**im***	הַבָּאִים
Egypt-ward	*Mitsraimah*	מִצְרָיְמָה
— (with) Jacob	*et Ya'akov*	אֵת יַעֲקֹב
(each) man and-house-his	*eesh oo-veito*	אִישׁ וּבֵיתוֹ
they came	*ba'oo*	בָּאוּ׃

—*Exodus 1:1*

Related Words

name	*shem*	שֵׁם
"the Name," God	*ha-**shem***	הַשֵּׁם
in the name of Yeshua	*b'**shem** Yeshua*	בְּשֵׁם יֵשׁוּעַ
good name, fame, reputation	*shem tov*	שֵׁם טוֹב
bad reputation, disrepute	*shem ra*	שֵׁם רָע
Thank God!, God be praised!	*baruch ha-**Shem***	בָּרוּךְ הַשֵּׁם
for heaven's sake	*l'**shem** shamayim*	לְשֵׁם שָׁמַיִם
to make a name for oneself	*asah lo shem*	עָשָׂה לוֹ שֵׁם

Hit the Trail!

A Nation from 70 Names

> **❝** *These are the names of the sons of Isra'el who came into Egypt with Ya'akov; each man with his household . . .* **❞**
>
> —*Exodus 1:1*

Sefer SH'MOT (*the book of Exodus/names*) starts with v' (the conjunction *and*), to stress continuity with Sefer B'REISHEET (*the book of Genesis/in the beginning*). In fact, the first six Hebrew words, v'eleh SH'MOT b'nei Yisra'el ha-ba'im Mitzraimah, correspond identically to a previous verse (Gen. 46:8). After this brief look backward to link the two books, we now can appreciate the forward progress in God's step-by-step plan to redeem mankind.

With the family united, the seventy souls "issuing from Ya'akov's loins" [Fox, Ex. 1:5] quickly multiply like swarming creatures (Ex. 1:7; Gen. 1:20) until the land of Goshen overflows. The sons of Yisra'el are fruitful, multiplying and filling the earth (Gen. 1:28, cf. Gen. 9:7).

With the family unified, God forges a nation.

Recall that Noach's seventy grew into the nations of the world (Gen. 10). Now Ya'akov's seventy grow rapidly into a nation that threatens Egypt, the world power (Ex. 1:1-9; Dt. 10:22)!

? *Read God's promises to greatly increase the descendants of the patriarchs (Gen. 17:1-8; 26:1-5; 28:13-15). Comment on how promises take up most of B'REISHEET, while their fulfillment flashes by in nine quick verses of SH'MOT!*

Moshe Rescued!

❝ *The king of Egypt summoned the midwives and demanded of them, "Why have you done this and let the boys live?"* ❞

—*Exodus 1:18*

Pharaoh tries to slow Yisra'el's population growth through slavery and harsh working conditions. When this plot fails, he calls on the Hebrew midwives to kill male newborns. The midwives "fear God" more than they fear Pharaoh, so they let the sons live (Ex. 1:17).

Women play a prominent role in saving the savior.

Pharaoh confronts the midwives, charging them with a felony [Childs, p. 17]. The midwives wittily reply that the Hebrew women are robust and vigorous, unlike the Egyptians, and they give birth before the midwives arrive.

Enraged, Pharaoh orders his entire population to drown Jewish baby boys in the deep of the Nile! Yet once again, a woman frustrates his plan. Ironically, Pharaoh's own daughter "draws out from the water" a Jewish baby boy, whom she names "Moshe" (Ex. 2:10). She calls a Hebrew midwife to nurse the infant— Moshe's very own mother (Ex. 2:7-8)!!

? *According to the Talmud, the astrologers warned Pharaoh that a savior was about to be born [Sot. 12b].*
• *Thus, Pharaoh attempted to kill Moshe as a baby. Read Matthew 2:1-20. Compare the accounts of Moshe and Yeshua.*

Wake-Up Call

❝ One day, when Moshe was a grown man, he went out to visit his kinsmen; and he watched them struggling at forced labor. He saw an Egyptian strike a Hebrew, one of his kinsmen. ❞—Exodus 2:11

At the age of 40, Moshe leaves the palace to look upon the sufferings of "his kinsmen" (Ac. 7:23; Heb. 11:24-25). Perhaps Moshe's compassion for the downtrodden had been taught to him by the careful watching of Tsiporah, Miryam, and Pharaoh's daughter, all of whom see and are moved by compassion (Ex. 2:2, 4, 5-6).

Here, Moshe looks upon the burdens of his brethren and likewise feels compassion (Ex. 2:11-12a, cf. 1:11). His going out is a purposeful seeking. Moshe intends to look upon his brothers' suffering and to grieve with them [Rashi]. The words "his kinsmen," used twice in Ex. 2:11, underscore Moshe's maturity and sensitivity, as he now identifies with his Jewish brothers.

Moshe looks upon his kinsmen's burdens.

In like manner, the LORD Himself looks upon the groanings of the sons of Yisra'el with paternal love (Ex. 2:24-25, cf. Ps. 31:7(8תה״ל)).

? *Read Hebrews 11:24-25. Explain what compels Moshe to choose mistreatment and affliction rather than to enjoy "the passing pleasures of sin."*

The Shepherd Sees

> ❝ Now Moshe was tending the sheep of Yitro his father-in-law, the priest of Midyan. Leading the flock to the far side of the desert, he came to the mountain of God, to Horev. ❞ —Exodus 3:1

Moshe stands at the mountain of God! To find this spot, "on the far side of the desert," required Moshe to search far and wide. The mere fact that Moshe oversees the flock so far from Yitro's camp shows great trust. The flock is literally "the ranch," Yitro's capital in toto.

Moshe is trusted with the sheep of his father-in-law.

According to Rashi, Chorev (*desolation*) and Har Sinai (*Mount Sinai*) depict the same spot. Here the shepherd sees a great sight—a bush "flaming with fire" (Ex. 3:3). The LORD appears and says, "I have surely seen the affliction of My people" (Ex. 3:7). The similar Hebrew forms of the underlined words playfully enhance this amazing picture.

The stage is set for the shepherd of Yitro's flock to return as shepherd of Yisra'el. Moshe's flock of two million will worship God at this very mountain (Ex. 3:12). Only next time, not a mere bush, but the entire mountain will be aflame—a great sight, indeed!

?
Read Mt. 6:4; 10:6. Moshe spends 40 obscure years, tending his father-in-law's sheep in the wilderness of Sinai.
• Then God brings the sons of Yisra'el to Sinai, and Moshe shepherds another 40 years in the same wilderness. Déjà vu??

Lead the Leaders!

> ❝ *Go, gather the leaders of Isra'el together, and say to them, "ADONAI, the God of your fathers . . . has appeared to me and said, 'I . . . have seen what is being done to you in Egypt . . . '"* ❞ —*Exodus 3:16*

Carry the message to the elders, the LORD tells Moshe, and the leaders will "sham'u l'kolecha (*listen to your voice*)" (Ex. 3:18; cf. Gen. 22:18 when Avraham listened to God's voice).

The LORD will account for His promises and oath.

Furthermore, Moshe is to tell Pharaoh that the God of the Hebrews wants a festival with offerings, "three days' journey" into the wilderness! The LORD promises to grant chen (*favor*) in the eyes of the Egyptians (Ex. 3:21).

Stunned, Moshe replies that the leaders won't listen to his voice and will retort, "ADONAI did not appear to you" (Ex. 4:1; cf. Gen. 18:1, 13 when the LORD appeared to Avraham but even Sarah had trouble believing).

However, the LORD is emphatic! He claims that Moshe will be as "God" to Pharaoh [Kaplan on Ex. 4:16]. "Pakod pakad'ti (*I have watched over you/accounted for your account*)," says the LORD (Ex. 3:16)—the same watchful accounting that Yosef assured his brothers God would grant as they awaited aliyah back to the Land (Gen. 50:24-25).

> **?** Re-read Gen. 22:18. The LORD promised Avraham an invincible seed, because Avraham listened to the LORD's voice and offered his son as an olah after three days' journey into the wilderness. What inheritance is promised?

Father-in-Law's Blessing

> ❝ *Moshe left, returned to Yitro his father-in-law and said to him, "I beg you to let me go and return to my kinsmen in Egypt, to see if they are still alive." Yitro said to Moshe, "Go in peace."* ❞ —*Exodus 4:18*

According to Rashi, Moshe promised Yitro he would stay. Thus, Moshe asks for permission to leave in order to be released from his word. Yitro's blessing to "go in peace" begins this segment (Ex. 4:18), whose central theme is "Send free my son that he might serve Me" (Ex. 4:23).

> **Yitro blesses Moshe and sends him free.**

What Pharaoh hardheartedly oppresses, Yitro blesses. No wonder the future portion bearing Yitro's name will contain the decalog, words of the covenant God speaks to the nation of Yisra'el.

Once released, Moshe journeys to Egypt. With Aharon at his side, Moshe performs signs and wonders given him by the LORD (cf. Jn. 20:31). The sons of Yisra'el immediately "believed," "heard that ADONAI had remembered (accounted for them)," "bowed," and "worshipped" (Ex. 4:31).

Thus, the father-in-law's blessing and the Father's concern (accounting) seal the seams of this segment.

> ❓ *Read Ex. 4:22-23. Yisra'el is God's firstborn son. The LORD sternly admonishes Pharaoh that He will kill his firstborn son if he refuses to let Yisra'el go. Relate God's warning to the idea of punishment, "measure for measure."*

Let My People Go!

> **"** After that, Moshe and Aharon came and said to Pharaoh, "Here is what ADONAI, the God of Isra'el, says: 'Let my people go so that they can celebrate a festival in the desert to honor me.'" **"** —*Exodus 5:1*

Moshe and Aharon repeat the LORD's word to Pharaoh. As predicted, Pharaoh retorts: "Who is ADONAI that eshma' b'kolo (*I should listen to His voice*)?" Pharaoh rubs in his words of defiance: "Lo yada'ti et- יהוה (*I do not know the LORD*), and I also won't let Yisra'el go" (Ex. 5:2).

The war of wills begins.

Once again, Moshe and Aharon make reference to a festival, three days' journey ba-midbar (*into the wilderness*).

Their plea falls on deaf ears (Ex. 5:3-4). Pharaoh responds by increasing the forced labor. Now the people must gather straw and still make the same quota of bricks (Ex. 5:17-19). As in the days of Moshe's infancy, Pharaoh takes the first step in the ruthless suppression of Yisra'el.

A war of wills begins. Will the sons of Yisra'el face another pogrom (Ex. 1:22; 5:21), or will Yisra'el be set free lishmo'a b'kolo (*to obey His voice*) and to journey three days to make offerings to the LORD (cf. Gen. 22:2-4, 17-18)?

? Carefully read Exodus 5:2-3. Compare and contrast Pharaoh's response to that of Moshe (Ex. 3:4, 11, 4:1, 10, 13, 19-20) and Avraham (Gen. 12:1-4, 22:1-3), after each one hears a word from the LORD.

The Mighty Hand of God

❝ *ADONAI said to Moshe, "Now you will see what I am going to do to Pharaoh. With a mighty hand he will send them off; with force he will drive them from the land!"* **❞**

—Exodus 6:1

Foremen of the people of Yisra'el confront Moshe and Aharon with the bitterness that Pharaoh has imposed upon them: "May ADONAI look at you and judge accordingly, because you have made us utterly abhorrent in the view of Pharaoh and his servants, and you have put a sword in their hands to kill us!" (Ex. 5:21).

Despondent, Moshe turns to the LORD and asks why the LORD's demands have only worsened an unbearable situation (Ex. 5:22-23).

Moshe knows Pharaoh will relent only if he is forced out by a stronger hand (Ex. 3:19). Indeed, Pharaoh's obduracy sets the stage for the LORD to multiply signs and wonders that will literally force Pharaoh to let Yisra'el go (Ex. 3:20).

> *The strong hand prevails in the war of wills.*

Now, the LORD makes the astonishing claim that He will use Pharaoh's very own hand to banish Yisra'el from Egypt (Ex. 6:1).

Meditate on the irony that the LORD will use Pharaoh's own hand to deliver Yisra'el. In what ways can the LORD deliver you from the might of the very thing oppressing you? from a desire to control? from a compulsion to win??

The Power of God   *Meander*

❝ *When his descendants see the work of my hands among them, they will consecrate my name. Yes, they will consecrate the Holy one of Ya'akov and stand in awe of the God of Isra'el.* ❞ —Isaiah 29:23

Mightier works of the hand of the LORD are now prophesied in order to redeem the fallen history of the sons of Ya'akov. Efrayim has lost his crown and the glory of leadership to Assyria (Is. 28:1-4).

> *Once again, delivered by the mighty hand of God.*

But the LORD, who "redeemed Avraham" when he was assimilating in Assyria (Is. 29:22) and delivered "the House of Ya'akov" from the power of Egypt, will act once more! The LORD's hand will work out a new redemption!

No longer will Ya'akov be embarrassed in the midst of the nations over his fallen holiness. "When his descendants see the work of <u>My hands</u> among them, they will consecrate . . . the Holy one of Ya'akov and stand in awe" (Is. 29:23). His redeemed children will be spoon-fed by the LORD (Is. 28:9-13).

Unlike Efrayim, the House of Ya'akov will be delivered from the perils of national assimilation and loss of covenant status.

? *Read Isaiah 28:11, 13. Who is taught "with stammering lips, in a foreign accent?" Who is given the word "precept by precept, line by line?" How does the LORD's hand redeem the foreign-born remnant of the House of Ya'akov?*

> **"** *. . . and the secrets of his heart are laid bare; so he falls on his face and worships God, saying, "God is really here among you!"* **"**
>
> — *1 Corinthians 14:25*

Up to now, foreign languages have been a sign of God's judgment. God created languages to divide the nations (Gen. 11:6-9), and even to judge Yisra'el among the Assyrians (the Haftarah, Is. 28:11-12).

Now, foreign languages are redeemed from their former role as a sign of God's judgment. All can glorify God together, each in his own tongue.

In the New Covenant, God chides Corinthians for child-like immaturity, particularly when they judge the intensity of their personal experience in worship as a sign of spiritual maturity (1 Cor. 3:2; 14:20; Carson, p. 108].

> *Prophecy makes known the power of God.*

Prophecy makes intelligible what tongues do not! In prophecy, secrets of the heart are laid bare, bringing the terrifying conviction that God dwells among His people (1 Cor. 14:25).

? Read Isaiah 45:14, 17. Egypt, as a nation, will prostrate themselves, saying, "Surely God is with you; there is no other, other gods are nothing." How does God's Presence through prophecy change the hearts of unbelievers?

Talk Your Walk . . .

Ya'akov journeys to Mitzrayim to join his family into God's "called out" household (Gen. 46:3, 27). The seventy sons "issuing from Ya'akov's loins" are destined to redeem the seventy sons of Noach, who have grown into the seventy nations of the world [Gen. 10:32; Stone, p. 47].

In the first seven verses of Sefer SH'MOT (*Book of Exodus/Names*), Ya'akov's united twelve-tribe household begins to fulfill the primordial, pre-fall command of the LORD to be fruitful, multiply, fill the earth, and subdue it (Gen. 1:28). The land of Goshen overflows with the sons of Yisra'el, threatening the empire of Mitzrayim (*Egypt*).

> *The LORD prepares Moshe to bring out His people.*

Pharaoh tries in vain to slow the growth. First, he imposes heavy labor upon the population. Next, he orders the midwives to kill the male children. When that fails, he orders the entire population to drown the babies in the Nile. But he is circumvented by women: Tsipporah, Miryam, midwives, and his own daughter!

Moshe learns compassion from these women. Though raised in the royal court, he identifies with his "underdog" brethren. God uses shepherding to prepare Moshe as leader. After a contest of wills with Pharaoh, Moshe will return to the very same desert with the lost sheep of the House of Yisra'el!

Oasis

. . . Walk Your Talk

Who is the LORD that eshma' b'kolo (*I should listen to his voice*)? The universe is framed on your answer to this question!

Avraham immediately saddled up and journeyed three days to offer up Yitzchak as an olah (*ascent offering, holocaust*). In the case of Avraham's obedience, God responded by promising an invincible nation that would redeem the world, ekev asher sh'mata b'koli (*as a result that you listened to My voice*)!

In contrast, Pharaoh defied God and restrained Yisra'el from going three days' journey to offer sacrifices in the wilderness. After pogroms to kill male infants and destroy a nation-in-embryo, Pharaoh now increases the severity of Yisra'el's slavery.

What is true for Avraham and for k'lal Yisra'el (*all of Israel*) is also true for you! God demands nothing less than that sh'mata b'kolo (*you listen to His voice*). You must listen and obey—it's the only way. Moreover, God will

> ### *Listen and obey—it's the only way.*

build on your obedience. Remember, it is impossible to outgive God! Does it arouse your curiosity to see how God will use your sacrifice to redeem the world?

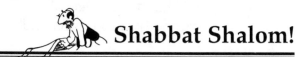

Shabbat Shalom!

And I appeared, וָאֵרָא,
to Moshe.
I spelled out My name:
yod-hay-vav-hay.
I said, "Prepare the leaders!
It's Redemption Day,
and signs and wonders
will lead the way!"

"Plagues of blood, frogs, lice
on a scale so grand,
I'll send hoards of beasts
to cover Egypt-land.
I'll sicken Pharaoh's cattle,
give him boils as planned,
and hurl mighty hail stones
that no tree can withstand!"

Walk VA'ERA!
6:2-9:35

ואָרֵא

And I appeared

TORAH—Exodus 6:2-9:35
  1st יהוה Appears—Exodus 6:2-3
  2nd Authorizing Spokesmen—Exodus 6:14, 26
  3rd "Speak to Pharaoh!"—Exodus 6:29
  4th Perform Signs and Wonders—Exodus 7:8-9
  5th First, God's Finger—Exodus 8:11(7תנצ"ך)
  6th Then, God's Hand—Exodus 8:23(19תנצ"ך)
  7th Slam the Land!—Exodus 9:17-18
  Maftir Strengthen Pharaoh's Heart—Exodus 9:35

HAFTARAH—Ezekiel 28:25-29:21
  Yisra'el Vindicated—Ezekiel 29:21

B'RIT CHADASHAH—Revelation 16:1-21
  Hail Slams the Nations—Revelation 16:21

And I Appeared,
Keeping Ancient Promises

Hiker's

← Looking Back

B 'REISHEET (*in the beginning*), God creates a perfect paradise. He places man in Gan Eden (*the Garden of Eden*), with the command to be fruitful, multiply, fill the earth, and subdue it.

> **B'REISHEET**—*in the beginning, God creates paradise and gives us free will. We choose disobedience and sibling rivalry. Quarrels finally resolve,* **VAY'CHI**—*and Ya'akov lives on through his children. These are their* **SH'MOT**—*names. Seventy go down to Egypt, multiply, and become enslaved. But God remembers us! "I AM* יהוה **VA'ERA**—*and I appeared"* *to keep My promise to Avraham.*

But man disobeys, and God banishes him from paradise, lest he eat of the Tree of Life and inherit eternal life. God appoints k'ruvim (*cherubim*) to guard the way to the Tree of Life.

NOACH (*Noah*) fathers a household, finds favor, and survives the flood. Ten evil generations pass. Then Avram (*exalted father*) is commanded, LECH L'CHA (*go forth, yourself!*) and start a new household, grounded in trust alone!

The household inherits the world's problems. Conflicts between brothers harden into fratricidal jealousies passed across generations, but finally solved in Yisra'el's family of twelve-sons. VAYIGASH Y'hudah (*and Judah drew near*), to repent for the grief he caused his father by selling brother Yosef into slavery. VAY'CHI Ya'akov (*and Jacob lived on*) through the lives of his children. So **Sefer B'REISHEET** (*the book of Genesis*) concludes in Egypt, with a reunified family and hopes for a return to the Land where the patriarchs rest.

Log

Sefer SH'MOT (*the book of Exodus/names*) reviews the journey of the sons of Yisra'el—each man and his household—to Egypt. V'eleh SH'MOT (*and these are the names*) of the seventy sons from the loins of Ya'akov, who embody the clan's hopes for nationhood. The family inherits the pre-fall blessings from God—to be fruitful, multiply, fill the earth, and subdue it—the exact promises God granted Adam and then Noach and his household.

But Pharaoh and his nation are threatened by these very promises. Yisra'el's growth is ruthlessly suppressed. Moshe himself is nearly drowned as an infant. Called by a burning bush later in life, Moshe is caught in a war of wills that pits God against Pharaoh. To fulfill ancient promises to

In VA'ERA . . .

The Key People are Moshe (*Moses*), Aharon (*Aaron*), Par'oh (*Pharaoh*), and the magicians.

The Scene is Mitzrayim (*Egypt*).

Main Events include God identifying Himself as יהוה—God of the covenant; Moshe's reluctance to lead; lineage cited to validate Moshe and Aharon; wonders performed with staff becoming snake; plagues of blood, frogs, lice, flies, cattle dying, and boils; Pharaoh's heart hardened first by self and later by God; plague of hail with warning to seek shelter; Pharaoh backing down, but only while under pressure, and then hardening his own heart again.

Avraham, God intervenes in human affairs. He tells Moshe: "VA'ERA (*and I appeared*)" as the LORD who is true to His word. Avraham's nation is destined to depart Egypt after 400 years of oppression . . .

The Trail Ahead ➡

The Path

וידבר אלהים אל משה
ויאמר אליו אני יהוה
וארא אל אברהם אל יצחק
ואל יעקב באל שׁדי
ושׁמי יהוה לא נודעתי להם

—שׁמות ו'/ב-ג—

וָ	אֶ	רְ	א
letter:	alef	reish	alef	vav
sound:	(silent)	**Rah**	(silent)'ei	Vah

and I appeared = VA Era = **וארא**

Work

The Legend

and spoke God	va-y'daber Elohim	וַיְדַבֵּר אֱלֹהִים
to Moses	el-Mosheh	אֶל־מֹשֶׁה
and He said unto him	va-yomer elav	וַיֹּאמֶר אֵלָיו
I am the Lord	ani **יהוה** (ADONAI)	אֲנִי יְהֹוָה׃
<u>and I appeared</u>	<u>va'era</u>	וָאֵרָא
to Abraham	el-Avraham	אֶל־אַבְרָהָם
to Isaac	el-Yitzchak	אֶל־יִצְחָק
and to Jacob	v'el Ya'akov	וְאֶל־יַעֲקֹב
as God Almighty	b'El Shaddai	בְּאֵל שַׁדָּי
& (but by) my name Lord	oo-sh'mi **יהוה** (ADONAI)	וּשְׁמִי יְהֹוָה
not was I known to them	lo noda'ti lahem	לֹא נוֹדַעְתִּי לָהֶם׃

—Exodus 6:2-3

Related Words

to see, look at, behold	ra-ah	רָאָה
to witness	ra-ah b—	רָאָה בְּ-
to be seen, appear, pretend, seem	nirah	נִרְאָה
exhibition, show	ra'avah	רַאֲוָה
See you again! (until seeing each other)	l'hitraot!	לְהִתְרָאוֹת!
and He appeared (Gen. 18:1)	va-yera	וַיֵּרָא

Hit the Trail!

יְהוָֹה Appears

> ❝ God spoke to Moshe . . . "I am ADONAI. I appeared to Avraham, Yitz'chak and Ya'akov as El Shaddai, although I did not make myself known to them by my name, Yud-Heh-Vav-Heh [ADONAI]. ❞ —Ex. 6:2-3

The patriarchs did not know ADONAI by the name יְהוָֹה (the LORD), because the time had not yet come to carry out the promises He'd made. The Lord prophesied to Avram that his seed would be redeemed, but first a nation had to be formed (Gen. 15:13-14).

And I appeared, to fulfill ancient promises.

Avraham, Yitzchak, and Ya'akov did know God by name (Gen. 15:1-2, 7; 26:2; 28:13, 16, 21). In fact, Ya'akov promises to worship Yud-Heh-Vav-Heh as his God upon returning safely to Beit-El (Gen. 28:21). Yet afterwards, the LORD calls Himself El Shaddai (Gen. 35:11-12; 48:3).

Knowing yet not knowing ADONAI's name seems contradictory to the western mind. But the patriarchs have not yet experienced ADONAI as the "One Who is faithful to verify His words" [Rashi]. First, the LORD must create a nation and then redeem it with a strong hand. ADONAI's personal appearance—VA'ERA—makes good on past promises!

? Read the promises of nationhood made to the patriarchs (Gen. 12:1-3; 17:5-8; 26:3-5; 28:13-15). Find the four cups of Passover plus the cup for Eliyahu in the verbs given in Exodus 6:6-8. Relate these cups to the promises of the LORD.

Authorizing Spokesmen

❝ *These were the heads of their families . . . These are the Aharon and Moshe to whom ADONAI said, "Bring the people of Isra'el out of the land of Egypt, division by division."* ❞   —*Exodus 6:14, 26*

Genealogy serves as an interlude between the narrative of the Rishon and Shlishi (*1st and 3rd sections*). This genealogy legitimates Moshe and Aharon as official representatives, authorized to speak the LORD's word to Pharaoh.

Moshe and Aharon are legitimated as spokesmen.

The genealogy is quite selective, narrowing on the lineage of Moshe and Aharon, to vouch for their authenticity as fourth generation sons of Levi. Torah spells out the longevity within this clan: Levi died at 137, his son K'hat died at 133, and Amram, Moshe and Aharon's father, died at 137 (Ex. 6:16, 18, 20).

It is singularly striking that no other ages are recorded, nor are any second or third generational names given for the other tribes named. Both Stone and Sforno observe that the Levites outlived their siblings and were able to spend quality time rearing and educating children and grandchildren for this day.

? *Read Exodus 6:26-28. Explain why the LORD speaks only to Moshe and Aharon. Also, why is it that ADONAI says to bring out the sons of Yisra'el "by their armies?"*

"Speak to Pharaoh!"

" . . . he said, "I am ADONAI. Tell Pharaoh, king of Egypt, everything I say to you." "

—*Exodus 6:29*

Exact wording at the end of the Rishon (*first section*) is repeated in the Shlishi (*third section*) to give continuity to the unfolding story line (Ex. 6:10-12, 29). In fact, these are the first two times that the LORD tells Moshe to tell Pharaoh, "everything 'I' say to you" (Ex. 6:29). The statement will be repeated seventy times in the Torah.

ADONAI says He is appointing Moshe as Elohim (God) to Pharaoh (Ex. 7:1). Moshe interrupts, saying he lacks the self confidence to speak for the LORD—that he is a man of uncircumcised lips. The LORD offers a solution. Aharon will speak for Moshe.

The LORD elevates Moshe, with Aharon as prophet.

The LORD reiterates that He will personally harden Pharaoh's heart (Ex. 7:3; 4:21). He purposes to multiply signs and wonders so that Yisra'el, Egypt, and all the world will come to know the LORD alone is ADONAI (Ex. 7:5). The liberation process will require exacting obedience on the part of Moshe and Aharon (Ex. 7:6).

? *Read Dt. 18:18-19. The sons of Yisra'el were told to look for a prophet through whom God would speak. Read Jn. 5:19-20, and explain Yeshua's role as God's prophet. How critical is it to speak the exact word of God?*

Perform Signs and Wonders

" ADONAI said to Moshe and Aharon, "When Pharaoh says to you, 'Perform a miracle,' tell Aharon to take his staff and throw it down in front of Pharaoh, so that it can become a snake." " —Exodus 7:8-9

Otot (*signs*) are performed to validate the authenticity of the messenger. Moftim (*wonders*) authenticate the greatness of the Sender [Sforno]. ADONAI performs signs for Yisra'el and wonders for Pharaoh.

> **God multiplies signs and wonders to show power.**

The LORD directs Moshe to say, "Shalach et ami v'ya'av-duni (*Let My people go that they may serve Me*)" (Ex. 7:16, 26). Recall Pharaoh's previous response: "Who is ADONAI that eshma b'kolo (*I should listen to His voice*)?" (Ex. 5:2).

Ten times will God command Moshe or Aharon to "stretch out his staff/hand" and perform wonders to authenticate His greatness to Pharaoh and his people.

Pharaoh resists, saying, "Perform <u>for your-selves</u> a wonder" (Ex. 7:9). God has anticipated Pharaoh's order. "Exactly as ADONAI has commanded" (Ex. 7:10), Aharon throws down the staff. Yet whatever the wonder—a rod to a snake, the Nile to blood—Pharaoh hardens. The battle lines form!

? *Read Ex. 7:5, 19; 8:5(1 תֵּנ"ך), 16(12 תֵּנ"ך); 9:22; 10:12, 21; 14:16, 26; 15:12. Fox [p. 291] observes the "hand" that is "stretched out" is not actually the LORD's (Ex. 7:4), but that of Moshe or Aharon! In light of Exodus 7:1, explain God's purpose.*

First, God's Finger

> **"** *". . . The frogs will leave you and your homes, also your servants and your people; they will stay in the river only."* **"**
>
> —*Exodus 8:11* (תנ״ך 7)

Plagues begin, and Pharaoh bargains for relief. As promised, the very next day the frogs return to the river. Yet Pharaoh sees the respite as weakness. He hardens his heart in response to the LORD's gracious answer to Moshe's prayer (Ex. 8:15(11 תנ״ך)). Of course, the LORD had also predicted Pharaoh's recalcitrance!

Again, the LORD directs Aharon to stretch forth his hand. Lice! Pharaoh's magicians are unable to copy this plague (Ex. 8:18(14 תנ״ך)). The magicians tell Pharaoh it is the etsba elohim (*finger of God*).

Again, Pharaoh hardens his heart, exactly as God had predicted (Ex. 8:19(15 תנ״ך)).

Pharaoh hardens himself against the finger of God.

God follows up with yet another warning for yet another plague. Again, Moshe is directed to repeat the purpose of the wonders: Shalach ami v'ya'avduni (*Let My people go that they may serve Me!*) (Ex. 8:20(16 תנ״ך)). The LORD will distinguish His people in Goshen, so the Egyptians will know that "I am ADONAI" (Ex. 8:22(18 תנ״ך)).

? *The eye of compassion views voluntary surrender as good will. The eye of power views the same respite as weakness! Explain how Moshe's compassionate response serves to harden a power-hungry tyrant.*

Then, God's Hand

❝ "'Yes, I will distinguish between my people and your people, and this sign will happen by tomorrow.'" ❞

—*Exodus 8:23 (19 תִּנָּ"ךְ)*

I will set a p'dut (*redemption*) between My people and your people," [Rashbam, Ibn Ezra on Ex. 8:23(19 תִּנָּ"ךְ)]. When the finger fails, God turns to the hand! God purposes to redeem His people.

> **God's hand of judgment inflicts severe pain.**

Accordingly, a great arov (*mixture*) of beasts, serpents, and wild animals attack the land of Egypt (Ex. 8:24(20 תִּנָּ"ךְ)). But Pharaoh resists!

Now distinctions are created between Israelite and Egyptian livestock. God's hand strikes the Egyptian livestock with illness (Ex. 9:3). Pharaoh hardens further!

In the sixth plague, God commands Moshe and Aharon to take a double handful of ashes and throw it in the air. Boils strike all Egyptians! Even the magicians can find no relief (Ex. 9:11). This time, God Himself "makes strong" Pharaoh's heart (Ex. 9:12). Sforno explains that severe bodily discomfort can break a person's free will (cf. Job 2:5). Thus, God strengthens a heart so it can continue to resist!

? *Read Ex. 8:25-27(21-23 תִּנָּ"ךְ). The Egyptians considered sheep sacred [Targ. Yonatan in Kaplan, p. 294; Rashi; Stone, p. 333]. How dangerous would it be for the sons of Yisra'el to slaughter sheep in the land of Egypt? Explain.*

Slam the Land!

> **❝ Since you are still setting yourself up against my people and not letting them go, tomorrow, about this time, I will cause a hailstorm so heavy that Egypt has had nothing like it . . . ❞** —*Exodus 9:17-18*

Because Pharaoh continues "lording it over" [Ibn Ezra, Radak] the sons of Yisra'el ("My people"), the LORD threatens the most frightening plague. Even the advance warning sounds off alarm bells when the LORD threatens to send all His plagues el lib'cha (*to your very heart*, Ex. 9:14).

It is as if all seven plagues hit at once! For the first time, Pharaoh has a moment of awareness that it is not Moshe, but the LORD God Who confronts him [Or HaChaim in Stone, p. 337].

Lightning fires the skies. The thunder, heard as the bat kol (*voice of the LORD*), scares Pharaoh most of all [Ber. 59a].

The 'voice of the LORD' causes Pharaoh to tremble.

For the first time, Pharaoh confesses, "This time I have sinned . . . I and my people are in the wrong" (Ex. 9:27). With his heart pounding in terror, Pharaoh calls Moshe and pleads for intercession (Ex. 9:28). Moshe promises to exit the city and pray for instant relief (Ex. 9:29).

? *Read Ex. 9:20-21, 25. Those who paid no attention to the dire warnings left servants and livestock in the fields, while others heeded the warnings and fled indoors. How does this plague prepare some Egyptians to leave Egypt?*

Strengthen Pharaoh's Heart

> **❝** *Pharaoh was made hardhearted, and he didn't let the people of Isra'el go, just as ADONAI had said through Moshe.* **❞**
>
> —*Exodus 9:35*

Again, God's compassion is treated as weakness. Moshe exits the city and spreads out his hands in intercession. Immediately the thunder, lightning, and hail cease.

Pharaoh responds instantly, by steeling his heart (Ex. 9:34). Thus, Torah states further, Pharaoh strengthened his heart (Ex. 9:35). Once more, Pharaoh has strengthened his own heart, the very moment that the thunder has stopped. To punctuate this idea further, Torah adds, ka'asher diber ADONAI b'yad Moshe (*just as* the LORD *had said by the hand of Moshe*, Ex. 9:35).

> *Pharaoh grows stronger in his ability to resist God.*

The maftir summarizes the effects of wonders. Pharaoh remains adamant about preventing God's son, Yisra'el, from leaving on a three-day journey to sacrifice to the LORD (Ex. 9:35). Therefore, the heart of Pharaoh is anaesthetized from the pain that his people are dying. The end of the confrontation draws near.

? *Review Ex. 3:18; 5:3; 8:23(27 תנ"ך). The contest pivots on whether Pharaoh will "let My people go" (Ex. 8:1-2 (7:26-27 תנ"ך); 8:8, 20, 21, 28, 29, 32 (8:4, 16, 17, 24, 25, 28 תנ"ך); 9:1, 2, 7, 8, 13, 17, 28, 35). What purpose is served by this war of wills?*

Yisra'el Vindicated   *Meander*

> ❝ *When that day comes I will cause power to return to the house of Isra'el, and I will enable you [Yechezk'el] to open your mouth among them. Then they will know that I am ADONAI."* ❞ — Ez. 29:21

In this reading, the LORD reacts even more strongly against the self deification of Pharaoh. Pharaoh claims to have formed the Nile (Ez. 29:3). Now the LORD will execute judgments upon Egypt, and "Then all who live in Egypt will know that I am ADONAI" (Ez. 29:6). In fact, Egypt's punishment will teach both Egypt and Yisra'el that the LORD is God (Ez. 29:9, 21).

Nebuchadnezzar will reduce Egypt to ruination, and never again will Egypt become a dominant world power (Ez. 29:15, 17-20).

History gives testimony to the truth of Ezekiel's prophecy. After a tidal wave robbed Nebuchadnezzar of all the booty he seized from Tyre, the king turned his rage upon Egypt. Never again has Egypt recovered her former glory as a world empire.

Egypt will lose power, and Yisra'el will grow strong.

Curiously, the Israelites find voice, as exiles and guests in Egypt. The Septuagint is written there and later read by the nations [Plaut, p. 136, n21].

Read Ez. 29:19-20; Is. 43:3. As a world empire, Egypt oppresses Yisra'el. Later, Egypt gives false comfort to Yisra'el against Babylon. Explain the reason God exacts from Egypt wages for Babylon and ransom for Yisra'el.

...ings   Hail Slams the Nations

> ❝ *"And huge seventy-pound hailstones fell on the people from the sky. But the people cursed God for the plague of hail, that it was such a terrible plague."* ❞
>
> — Revelation 16:21

Hail at the end of days follows the pattern of past times of judgment. The plague to fall on Egypt was a hailstorm more severe than anything ever witnessed since the founding of Egypt (Ex. 9:24). In the aftermath, Egyptian courtiers begged Pharaoh to capitulate, saying Egypt is ruined (Ex. 10:7).

Revelation describes God's judgment on the ruling nation during the end of days. Again, an awesome hailstorm comes as the seventh plague. It rips the empire, resulting in the same pattern of "flashes of lightning, voices and peals of thunder . . . and a massive earthquake, (cf. the earthquake in the day of Yeshua), such as has never occurred since mankind has been on earth" (Rev. 16:18).

Man curses God for throwing down hailstones.

Alas, the results are the same as well. In all three of the final plagues, people curse God and harden their hearts (Rev. 16:9, 11, 21).

Study Ex. 9:24; Josh. 10:11; Is. 28:2, 17; Ez. 38:22; Rev. 11:19, 16:18-21. In each instance, hail symbolizes wrath—a great shaking of land with torrential rains and giant hailstones! Explain man's reaction to God's wrath.

Talk Your Walk . . .

ADONAI announces, "VA'ERA (*and I appeared*)" in order to fulfill ancient promises, to redeem Yisra'el from a nation that would enslave them. The LORD raises up Moshe and Aharon to speak for Him. Their Levitical credentials are spelled out, to the fourth generation. Moshe is elevated to the status of elohim (*god, judge*) before Pharaoh.

Aharon becomes Moshe's prophet and official spokesman to Pharaoh; and God directs the brothers to perform signs and wonders, to authenticate their veracity and show His power. God prophesies in advance that Pharaoh will resist. It is not surprising, then, when Pharaoh asks, "Who is God that I should know Him?" or "Perform for yourselves a wonder!"

The war of wills between God and Pharaoh pivots on whether or not Yisra'el can go on a three-day journey into the wilderness to serve Him. Pharaoh says no! The LORD responds by multiplying wonders, which gradually increase in intensity and force. At first, Pharaoh's magicians can somewhat copy the divine wonders; but

> *Pharaoh defies God's will, refusing to let Yisra'el go.*

eventually they surrender, telling Pharaoh that the LORD's finger is at work. God's hand further increases the plagues' intensity. Sometimes, God strengthens Pharaoh so he has the ability to resist. Finally, God's voice causes Pharaoh to panic, but Pharaoh strengthens his will to resist for the last time.

Oasis

. . . Walk Your Talk

W^e all have areas in our lives where we refuse to relinquish control to God. Pharaoh was rightly suspicious that his slave force would not return to Egyptian bondage, if he released them to go on a three-day journey into the wilderness to worship the LORD.

Pharaoh resisted allowing his slave force to walk out, because loss of the slave force would mean precipitous changes for the Egyptian way of life. Pharaoh knew that a change in the order of Egyptian stability could end his dynasty! Pharaoh had to retain power—his taste for power would not allow any alternative!

Coping requires a willingness to change one's tastes! Ask yourself, spiritually speaking, what you feed on. Is it acceptance from others? Is it admiration? Is it power to influence? Is it a desire to be important in someone else's eyes? Is it a desire to do something important for God?

You must become transparently honest with

> *Your addictions shape your decisions, and your decisions shape your life.*

yourself. If you are fooling yourself, you cannot even pray for a change in your tastes. Yet, above all, you must develop a taste for always pleasing the LORD. You must taste and see that the LORD is good.

Shabbat Shalom!

God told Moshe,
"בא!—go negotiate!
Get My people
OUT!
With locusts he'll bumble,
in darkness he'll stumble,
then Pharaoh will crumble,
NO DOUBT!"

Three times
God hardened Pharaoh's heart,
and Pharaoh said,
"No deal!"
Until his first-born died
and the people cried,
"Take our gold! Leave in peace!
God is real!!!"

Walk Bo!
10:1-13:16

Enter!

TORAH—Exodus 10:1-13:16

   1st Come, Mock Pharaoh!—Exodus 10:1
   2nd Painted Black!—Exodus 10:12
   3rd Conditions from Pharaoh—Exodus 10:24
   4th Judgment from the LORD—Exodus 11:4-5a
   5th It's You or the Lamb—Exodus 12:21
   6th A Nation is Judged—Exodus 12:29
   7th Ransom Complete—Exodus 13:1-2
   Maftir Redeemed from Egypt—Exodus 13:16

HAFTARAH—Jeremiah 46:13-28

   Just Punishment—Jeremiah 46:28

B'RIT CHADASHAH—Romans 9:14-29

   Righteous Mercy!—Romans 9:29

Enter . . . the Path to Freedom

Looking Back

B'Reisheet (*in the beginning*), God creates a perfect paradise. He places man in Gan Eden (*the Garden of Eden*), with the command to be fruitful, multiply, fill the earth, and subdue it.

> B'Reisheet,
> *God creates paradise.*
> vaY'chi *Ya'akov through his sons,*
> *and these are their* Sh'mot.
> *Seventy go down to Egypt,*
> *multiply, and become slaves.*
> *But God doesn't forget them!*
> *"I* am יהוה
> va'Era—*and I appeared"*
> *to keep My promise to Avraham.*
> *Now* Bo—*enter negotiations*
> *with Pharaoh*
> *to let My people go!*

This command is reiterated to Noach after the flood, and once again to the Sh'mot (*names*) of the sons of Yisra'el who, along with their households, journey down to Egypt to unify as a royal family.

The seventy sons of Yisra'el are immensely fruitful in Egypt. They multiply, fill Goshen, and begin to pose a threat to Mitzrayim (*Egypt*) itself. Pharaoh tries to slow the growth of the population by imposing harsh conditions of slavery. When this fails, Pharaoh orders the midwives to kill male newborns. Ironically, Moshe is named "pulled out " by Pharaoh's own daughter, who rescues the baby from drowning in the Nile.

A generation passes as Moshe is raised in Pharaoh's house. The cycle of suppression continues, and one day Moshe looks with compassion on the burdens of his brethren. He kills an Egyptian and then is forced to flee for yet another generation. But when Moshe is 80, God appears in a burning bush at Mount Sinai and

Log

tells him to return to Egypt to free his people.

God assures Moshe: VA'ERA (*and I appeared*) as the LORD in order to make good on promises to the fathers. He told Avram that his nation would be oppressed as slaves in a foreign land, but He also promised to punish the nation that enslaves them. Now, God appears as the One who keeps His word. He raises up Moshe and Aharon to make His name known to Yisra'el and to the nations of the world. They perform signs and wonders to free the people. Seven plagues are performed, but Pharaoh resists freeing Yisra'el.

Continuing the push for freedom, God tells Moshe: **BO** (*enter!*) and make final negotiations with Pharaoh to free the sons of Yisra'el with a mighty hand ...

In BO ...

The Key People are Moshe (*Moses*), Aharon (*Aaron*), Par'oh (*Pharaoh*), Par'oh's servants, Egyptians, and Israelites (about 600,000 men, 2 million total).

The Scene is Mitzrayim (*Egypt*), with a journey from Ra'amses (*Rameses*) to Sukkot (*Succoth*).

Main Events include the plagues of locusts and darkness, affecting Egyptians but not Israelites; first passover with blood on the doorposts, to be observed yearly with matzah; death of Egyptian firstborns, with Pharaoh kicking out the Israelites; Egyptians urging haste and giving away plunder; Israelites journeying out, exactly 430 years after God prophesied that Avraham's seed would be strangers, enslaved and oppressed; and finally, the firstborns being set apart for God.

The Trail Ahead

Compass

The Path

ויאמר יהוה אל משה
בא אל פרעה
כי אני הכבדתי את לבו
ואת לב עבדיו
למען שתי אתתי אלה בקרבו

—שמות י׳/א

	א	בֹּ
letter:	alef	bet
sound:	(silent)	**Bo**

enter! = **Bo** = **בֹּא**

Work

The Legend

and said the LORD	va-*yomer* ADONAI	וַיֹּאמֶר יְהוָֹה
to Moses	el-*Mosheh*	אֶל־מֹשֶׁה
enter! (go!) to Pharaoh	**bo** el-Par'*oh*	בֹּא אֶל־פַּרְעֹה
because I	ki-*Ani*	כִּי־אֲנִי הִכְבַּדְתִּי
hardened — heart-his	hich'**bad**'ti et-libo	אֶת־לִבּוֹ
and — heart servants-his	v'et-**lev** avadav	וְאֶת־לֵב עֲבָדָיו
so that I may perform	l'**ma'an** shiti	לְמַעַן שִׁתִי
signs-My, these,	oto**tai** eleh	אֹתֹתַי אֵלֶּה
in nearness-his	b'kirbo	בְּקִרְבּוֹ:

—*Exodus 10:1*

Related Words

come, arrive, enter	ba	בָּא
enter into a covenant, make an agreement	ba bi-*vrit*	בָּא בִּבְרִית
negotiate (to enter into words with him)	ba bi-dvarim imo	בָּא בִּדְבָרִים עִמּוֹ
welcome! (blessed is the one who comes)	baruch ha-**ba**	בָּרוּךְ הַבָּא
next year (the year the coming)	la-shanah ha-baah	לַשָּׁנָה הַבָּאָה
to be born (come to the world)	ba la-olam	בָּא לָעוֹלָם
the world to come	ha-olam ha-ba	הָעוֹלָם הַבָּא

Hit the Trail!

Come, Mock Pharaoh!

❝ ADONAI said to Moshe, "Go to Pharaoh, for I have made him and his servants hardhearted, so that I can demonstrate these signs of mine among them . . . " ❞
—Exodus 10:1

Mockery! The LORD sends Moshe to confront the hardened heart of Pharaoh! God's purpose is two-fold: that certain Egyptians might repent and that the sons of Yisra'el will relate the exodus story to future generations [Sforno]. The story includes God's words: hit'allalti b'Mitzrayim (*I made sport of/made a mockery of Egypt*) [Ex. 10:2; Rashi, 1995, p. 92; Stone, p. 341].

The frantic Egyptian courtiers urge release, saying Egypt is ruined (Ex. 10:7). But instead, Pharaoh imposes conditions! Only the men might journey three days to worship the LORD (Ex. 10:8, 11).

Pressure on Pharaoh mounts.

Moshe is summarily expelled from the face of Pharoah (Ex. 10:11). This sets the stage for the final showdown between the LORD, who is showing His power, and Pharaoh, who is being strengthened to give flint-faced resistance to the signs and wonders of the LORD.

❓ Read Exodus 10:2. Plaut [p. 454] observes that the Passover story is related to the children so that the parents (not the sons!) might know that God is the LORD. Explain. What makes a story credible to others?

Painted Black!

❝ ADONAI said to Moshe, "Reach out your hand over the land of Egypt, so that locusts will invade the land and eat every plant that the hail has left." ❞
                                  —Exodus 10:12

Measure for measure, the punishments begin. Through the hand of Moshe, the staff of judgment is raised (Ex. 10:13).

> **Measure for measure, the LORD judges Egypt.**

Desert winds bring locusts so thick that they blacken the ground (Ex.10:15). Pharaoh pleads, ". . . remove this death from me!" [Fox, Ex. 10:17]. Even as the Egyptians had forced the Israelites to grow crops, now the locusts devour the crops. Moshe prays and the plague is reversed—a westerly wind dumps the locusts into the sea. Immediately, Pharaoh is strengthened to resist once more (Ex. 10:20).

The next plague is aimed at the Egyptian sun god, Amon-Re. This god is the source of heat, light, and creativity—the very symbol of cosmic order in Egypt. This time, Moshe extends his hand without the staff (Ex.10:21-22; cf. Ex. 9:23, 10:13). A darkness descends, so tangible it could be felt! No one could move for three days!

? *Read Ex. 3:18, 5:3, 8:27(23 ךְ"נֹת), 10:22-23. Do you think withholding the children of Yisra'el from a three-day festival to the LORD is punished—measure for measure—by three days of darkness in Egypt? What festival follows?*

Conditions from Pharaoh

> ❝ *Pharaoh summoned Moshe and said, "Go, worship* Adonai; *only leave your flocks and herds behind—your children may go with you."* ❞
>
> —*Exodus 10:24*

Now, even the children can go on the three-day journey! Yet, Pharaoh imposes conditions: "Go, worship Adonai; only leave your flocks and herds behind" (Ex. 10:24).

Pharaoh defies God with conditions and threats.

Obviously, this condition puts a dampener on what the Lord requires for sacrifice. Moshe responds that Pharaoh must provide the z'vachim v'olot (*festal sacrifices and ascent offerings*, Ex. 10:25).

As the confrontation comes to a head, Pharaoh threatens, "Get away from me! And you had better not see my face again, because the day you see my face, you will die!" (Ex. 10:28). This brutal death threat turns out to be Pharaoh's final condition.

Measure for measure, Pharaoh will reap what he has sown. Egypt will lose both its firstborn sons and its cattle. Tradition observes that the wicked do not repent, even on the threshold of destruction [Eruvin 19a].

? Read Gen. 15:14, Ex. 11:2-3, and Dt. 15:13. *Explain why God granted chen (favor) so the Egyptians would give up their riches. How does this relate to the chen Ya'akov received when repaying his brother Esav (Gen. 33:10-11)?*

Judgment from the LORD

" Moshe said, "Here is what ADONAI says: 'About midnight I will go out into Egypt, and all the first-born in the land of Egypt will die . . . "
—*Exodus 11:4-5a*

God personally goes into Egypt to slay Egypt's first-borns—both men and livestock (Ex. 11:4, 12:12). Slaying livestock includes killing key symbols of divinity in Egypt—the bulls of Apis and the cows of Hathor [Cassuto, p. 135]. The LORD will execute judgments on all the gods of Egypt (12:12).

Fox [p. 313] observes that the cry of the Egyptians on midnight will echo the cries of the sons of Yisra'el under the yoke of slavery (Ex. 3:7, 9). God's patience has limits. When grace finally runs its course, God repays measure for measure.

God announces judgment upon Egypt and its gods.

The retribution for Pharaoh's ruthlessness is also matched, measure for measure. Moshe responds to Pharaoh in the most prophetic of words, "All your servants will come down to me, prostrate themselves before me and say, 'Get out!—you and all the people who follow you!' and after that, I will go out!" (Ex. 11:8).

Read Exodus 12:3-4. Explain why households and not persons are redeemed by the blood of the lamb. Explain how the blood of the lamb on the lintel could protect the firstborns of two households that combined to share a lamb.

It's You or the Lamb

❝ Then Moshe called for all the leaders of Isra'el and said, "Select and take lambs for your families, and slaughter the Pesach lamb . . ." ❞

—Exodus 12:21

Leaders are ordered to slaughter the Passover lamb for their respective households. In this way, each clan could verify that its families were protected by the blood of the lamb (Ex. 12:3, 6).

Yisra'el is told to kill or be killed.

The statute was obeyed ka'asher tsivah ADONAI et Moshe (*exactly as the LORD commanded Moshe*, Ex. 12:28). Its memory is to be relived from generation to generation without end (Ex. 12:24).

At Passover, the children of the house ask, "What is this avodah (*service*) which you do?" The father's duty is to remind them that God struck the Egyptians, but he passed over <u>our</u> houses (Ex. 12:26-27).

Vicarious appropriation of experience creates the experience anew, making the past present. The zevach-pesach (*Passover festal sacrifice*) is the LORD's sign of redemption to the sons of Yisra'el (Ex. 12:27). Avodah (*work*), once compelled by force in slavery, is now redeemed as a *service* offered up freely to the LORD.

? Shemot R. 10:2 quoted in Leibowitz [p. 195] says, " . . . take you a lamb, and slaughter thereby the gods of Egypt and make the Passover." Sheep were worshiped in Egypt. What could happen to someone who slaughtered a lamb?

A Nation is Judged

❝ At midnight ADONAI killed all the firstborn in the land of Egypt, from the firstborn of Pharaoh sitting on his throne to the firstborn of the prisoner in the dungeon, and all the firstborn of livestock. ❞   —Exodus 12:29

Midnight comes, and the LORD Himself strikes down the firstborns of Egypt. True to Moshe's word, Pharaoh is driven to immediate action by a grief-stricken nation. That night, the sons of Yisra'el are banished by Pharaoh's hand!

The LORD uses Pharaoh's hand to set Yisra'el free.

Pharaoh's reaction is halting and spasmodic: Get up! Leave! Go Worship! Take your cattle, too! According to your words! And bless me, too (Ex. 12:31-32). Every precondition and every hint of control is gone from Pharaoh's word. The people of Yisra'el request gold, silver, and clothing from their Egyptian neighbors, and Egypt is plundered (Ex. 12:35-36, cf. Ex. 3:22).

True to His word, God has given the children of Yisra'el grace in the eyes of the Egyptians, and they do not leave empty-handed (Dt. 15:13-14; Gen. 15:13-14). Rather, Yisra'el is set apart to God as a bond-servant set free! In the same moment, one nation is judged and another is redeemed!

?   Read Ex. 12:41: "Miketz (at the end of) 430 years, all the divisions of ADONAI left the land of Egypt." Explain how this relates to Gen. 41:1, Miketz (at the end of) 2 years, when Yosef is given gold, clothed, and set free to rule Egypt.

Ransom Complete

❝ ADONAI said to Moshe, "Set aside for me all the firstborn. Whatever is first from the womb among the people of Isra'el, both of humans and of animals, belongs to me." ❞
—*Exodus 13:1-2*

Firstborns are now sanctified, set apart from Egypt to serve the LORD. The LORD's words, Shalach et ami v'ya'avduni (*Let My people go that they might serve Me*), shake the empire of Egypt.

> **Passover re-enacts the ransom of the firstborns.**

The living memory of this exodus (Greek for "the way out") is re-enacted annually at Passover: "Remember this day, on which you left Egypt, mi-beit avadim (*from the house of work/bondage*), ki b'chozek yad (*because with a strong hand*) hotsi' ADONAI etchem mi-zeh (*brings out the LORD all of you from this*, Ex. 13:3).

The LORD further commands Yisra'el, v'avadata et ha'avodah ha-zot (*and you shall serve this service*, Ex. 13:5)—for seven days, no chametz (*leavening*) is to be eaten—and the seventh day shall be a holy convocation, a chag l'ADONAI (*festival to the LORD*, Ex. 13:6).

With the ransom of the firstborns complete, the LORD proclaims that all firstborn humans and livestock belong to Him (Ex. 13:1-2).

> ❓ *Read Gen. 5:29. Explain Lemech's hope for relief from the fall when he names his firstborn Noach: "This one will comfort us in our labor, in the hard work we do with our hands [to get . . .] from the ground that ADONAI cursed."*

Redeemed from Egypt

❝ This will serve as a sign on your hand and at the front of a headband around your forehead that with a strong hand ADONAI brought us out of Egypt. ❞

—Exodus 13:16

The sons of Yisra'el take most seriously the obligation to kadesh li (*sanctify to Me*) the firstborns.

> **Wear t'fillin to know that God brought His son out.**

These very words (Ex. 13:1-10) are written by hand on parchment, inserted into t'fillin (*prayer boxes*), and wrapped daily around the arm and head as a living memorial of the ransom completed (Ex.13: 11-16; Is. 43:3-4).

The pidyon ha-ben (*redemption of the son*) is observed on the thirtieth day of a firstborn's life. The infant is formally redeemed from the LORD to whom he belongs (Num. 3:45-47) by the payment of silver or ts'dakah (*charitable contributions*).

Avodah (*work*) by the sweat of one's brow (Gen. 3:17) is elevated, or transformed, to a *service of worship* which moves progressively in the direction of the avodah of Gan Eden (*the Garden of Eden*). For there, the LORD placed man in Paradise l'avdahh v'shamrahh (*to work it and watch over it*, Gen. 2:15).

Read Genesis 2:15, 3:17b, Ex.4:23; 6:6-8. Man's avodah (work/service/worship) is being transformed by God's saving acts. Explain how re-enacting the Passover story and putting on t'fillin points to a renewed future in Gan Eden.

Just Punishment   *Meander*

> 66 *"Don't be afraid, Ya'akov my servant,"* says
> *Adonai, "for I am with you. I will finish off all the
> nations where I have scattered you. However, you I
> will not finish off . . .* 99   — *Jeremiah 46:28*

Punishment upon Egypt is progressive. Here, the prophet Yirm'yahu prophesies that Pharaoh will fail to defeat Babylon at Carchemish on the Euphrates (605 BCE, about eight centuries after the exodus).

Egypt will diminish, because of idolatry.

Egypt is competing for world dominion with Babylon. Yirm'yahu warns that King Nebuchadrezzar is coming to strike the land of Egypt and <u>forever</u> prevent Egypt from again becoming a world power. Once and for all, Egypt must be punished for the sin of idolatry.

Amon-Re (still the head of the pantheon and special god of Egypt's rulers) must be destroyed forever (Nah. 3:8; Jer. 46:25). The good news is that Egypt will be restored after being crushed by Babylon (Ez. 29:13-16). In the end, the LORD promises mercy to Egypt, along with the other nations, Moab and Ammon. "Be not afraid," God counsels Yisra'el (Jer. 46:28).

? Read Isaiah 43:3. Explain how God has given Egypt as "the ransom" of Yisra'el. What does God mean when he says, "For you I will give people, nations in exchange for your life" (Is. 43:4)?

> ❝ *Also, as Yesha'yahu said earlier, "If* ADONAI-*Tsva'ot had not left us a seed, we would have become like S'dom. We would have resembled 'Amora."* ❞
> —*Romans 9:29*

Rav Sha'ul addresses the LORD's methods and purposes for redeeming mankind:

(1) Can God be righteous and show favoritism? (Ro. 9:14-15)

> **God saves man with compassion and righteousness.**

(2) If God hardens whom He pleases, then why does He still find fault, for who is able to resist His will? (Ro. 9:19)

(3) Does man really have a right to ask, "Why did you make me this way?" (Ro. 9:20)

(4) Can God just conclude and "cut things short," doing so in righteousness? (Ro. 9:28)

Rav Sha'ul answers:

(1) God manifests mercy. This is not unrighteousness (Ex. 9:16 in Ro. 9:17)

(2) Granted, no one can resist His will—not even Pharaoh (Ex. 9:12; 10:20, 27; 11:10).

(3) But it's patently absurd to criticize the Creator. Man is a mere pot (plasma, in Greek), without arms (Is. 45:9).

(4) God can judge the world for evil, save some (Ro. 9:24), "cut short" the rest (Is. 10:23; Ro. 9:28), and still manifest compassion with righteousness (Ro. 9:29; Is. 1:9; 13:19).

> ❓ *Compare Luke 17:26-29 with Romans 9:29. Yeshua relates the Days of Noach (Gen. 6-7) to the day Lot escaped S'dom (Gen. 18-19). In each, the* LORD *saves "seed." Discuss righteousness with compassion.*

Talk Your Walk . . .

Pharaoh has passed the point of no return in using his free will to resist God's will. The last three plagues, the LORD strengthens Pharaoh's ability to resist. In this way, Pharaoh is hardened for judgment. Measure for measure, God metes out His judgment upon Egypt. The conditions that Pharaoh imposes (leave the children, leave the cattle, a death threat to Moshe for his warnings) will boomerang upon Egypt. It is Egypt's sons, Egypt's cattle, and Pharaoh's own son who will be judged! At the national level, Yisra'el is God's firstborn son; so Egypt will be judged, losing its firstborns, both cattle and sons.

Also, Egypt's gods will be judged, including the incarnate god to succeed Pharaoh, his firstborn son! But one nation's judgment is another nation's redemption! Yisra'el is sanctified, set apart for God. The slaves who worked Pharaoh's crops are suddenly redeemed to worship the LORD. Thus, avodah (*work, service, worship*) is transformed in the life of Yisra'el. The nation moves one step closer to Gan Eden, where all work was a service of worship, holy to the LORD.

> *Judgment and redemption come at the same moment.*

With the ransom complete, the LORD proclaims that all Yisra'el's firstborns, men and livestock, belong to Him. Pidyon ha-ben (*redemption of the son*) is set aside as a day when firstborns are formally redeemed by payment of silver to the House of the LORD.

Oasis

. . . Walk Your Talk

Y ou have been redeemed with a price. This is why we recline, as free men do, during the Passover meal. This is also why we give shekels to the synagogue at the pidyon ha-ben ceremony for the firstborns. And for believers, you also know that the pouring out of Messiah's life means that your life has been purchased with blood. You are the firstfruits to be ransomed from death. But now, you belong to Him. There is no pidyon ha-ben for believers. Therefore, you must allow Him to live out His life in you. His body was given that you might live. Now, you must serve Him. Your life is a service of worship, and you have become His bond servant.

Your spiritual death in this life is real. The work you would have chosen for yourself must change in ways that suit His preferences. Your innermost circle for decision making must include God and no one else! He calls you His friend, and He has given you freedom to choose.

> *Redeemed with a price, you must decrease that He may increase in your life.*

He makes His preferences real in your life only if your tastes are, first and foremost, to serve Him with abiding joy. Are you ready to walk in a way that makes Him so alive in your life that you forget who you are?

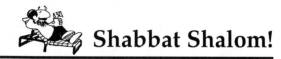 **Shabbat Shalom!**

Now בשלח says,
"When Pharaoh let go,"
God led us afar
from Philistine foe.
But Pharaoh came a-chasing
and we trembled, "Oooooh NO!"
How the sea split open,
we just dunno!

Yisra'el walked safely
across on dry ground.
The sea closed behind us,
the chariots drowned.
We sang to ADONAI,
gathered mannah all around,
until war with Am'lek
meant enemies surround!

Walk B'SHALACH!
13:17-17:16

בְּשַׁלַּח

When he let go

TORAH—Exodus 13:17-17:16
- 1st Evil Lets Go—Exodus 13:17
- 2nd The Army Pursues—Exodus 14:9
- 3rd Part the Sea!—Exodus 14:15-16a
- 4th Drown the Army!—Exodus 14:26
- 5th Living Water—Exodus 15:27
- 6th Bread from Heaven—Exodus 16:11-12
- 7th Test and Be Tested—Exodus 17:1
- Maftir War with Evil—Exodus 17:15-16

HAFTARAH—Judges 4:4-5:31
- Destroy All Evil!—Judges 5:31

B'RIT CHADASHAH—Revelation 19:1-20:6
- A Thousand-Year Peace!—Revelation 20:6

When Pharaoh Let Go, Yisra'el Grew Up

Looking Back

B'REISHEET (*in the beginning*), God creates a perfect paradise. He places man in Gan Eden (*the Garden of Eden*), to work the garden and watch over it. But man disobeys and is banished from perfect paradise.

Much later, God calls Avraham to a three-day journey into the wilderness. Avraham leaves the next day! For his obedience, he receives a promise that his son will father a nation that will overcome all enemies.

The book of Exodus begins by listing the **SH'MOT** (*names*) of the sons of Yisra'el, along with their households, who journey to Egypt to become the promised nation. These seventy sons of Yisra'el are immensely fruitful. Pharaoh tries to slow population growth by imposing the harsh work of slavery. God

had warned that our nation was destined to be enslaved, but He also promised a great redemption from this fate.

These are the SH'MOT of the sons of Yisra'el, suffering as slaves in Egypt. But God hasn't forgotten: VA'ERA to keep My promises. BO, negotiate to let My people go! B'SHALACH Pharaoh, God leads us out with a mighty hand!

God assures Moshe one day, VA'ERA (*and I appeared*) as ADONAI—the One who always keeps His word. The LORD raises up Moshe and Aharon to perform signs and wonders to free the people. Seven plagues are performed, but Pharaoh hardens.

God further instructs Moshe, **BO** (*enter!*) and negotiate with Pharaoh, to free the sons of Yisra'el with a mighty hand. Pharaoh tries to prevent

Log

Yisra'el from leaving, to go three days into the wilderness to worship the LORD. Movement is restricted—first, no one may go, then the children must remain, and finally the cattle. Measure for measure, Pharaoh is punished, and Yisra'el is thrust out by Pharaoh's own hand!

The fathers are commanded to eat matzah and recount the Exodus every year at Passover—a story of redemption, when God elevates the imposed work of slavery to a freely given service of love. True to His word, God redeems us so we can re-enter Gan Eden.

B'SHALACH Par'oh (*when Pharaoh let go*), God leads Yisra'el to freedom with an upraised hand . . .

In B'SHALACH . . .

The Key People are Par'oh (*Pharaoh*), the Israelites, Moshe (*Moses*), 600 Egyptians on chariots, Miryam (*Miriam*), Amalek, Y'hoshua (*Joshua*), Aharon (*Aaron*), and Hur.

The Scenes include the wilderness of the Red Sea, Sukkot to Eitam (*Succoth* to *Etham*), Pi haChirot (*Pi-hahiroth*) before Ba'al Ts'fon (*Baal Zephon*) by the sea, wilderness of Shur, Marah, Elim, wilderness of Sin, R'fidim (*Rephidim*), Chorev (*Horeb*), Massah and M'rivah (*Meribah*)

Main Events include Moshe carrying out Yosef's bones, pillars of cloud and fire; chariot chase, parting of the sea, Song of Moshe; bitter waters sweetened; mannah and quail, water from rock; fight against Amalek as Moshe holds up arms, Amalek remains Yisra'el's enemy.

The Trail Ahead

Compass

The Path

ויהי בשלח פרעה את העם
ולא נחם אלהים דרך
ארץ פלשתים כי קרוב הוא
כי אמר אלהים פן ינחם העם
בראתם מלחמה ושבו מצרימה

—שמות יג/יז

	ח	ל	שַׁ	בְּ
letter:	chet	lahmed	shin	bet
sound:	CH	Llah	SHah	B'

when he let go = B'SHALACH = בְּשַׁלַח

Work

and it was	va-y'**hi**	וַיְהִי
<u>when let go</u> Pharaoh	b'**shalach** Par'oh	בְּשַׁלַּח פַּרְעֹה
— the people	et-ha-**am**	אֶת־הָעָם
& not lead them God	v'lo-nacham Elohim	וְלֹא־נָחָם אֱלֹהִים
way of land of Philistines	derech eretz P'lishtim	דֶּרֶךְ אֶרֶץ פְּלִשְׁתִּים
because near he/it (was)	ki karov hoo	כִּי קָרוֹב הוּא
for said God	ki amar Elohim	כִּי אָמַר אֱלֹהִים
lest regret the people	pen-yinachem ha-**am**	פֶּן־יִנָּחֵם הָעָם
in seeing-their war	bir'otam mil'chamah	בִּרְאֹתָם מִלְחָמָה
& return Egypt-ward	v'shavu mitsraimah	וְשָׁבוּ מִצְרָיְמָה׃

—Exodus 13:17

Related Words

to send, dispatch, trans- mit, dismiss, drive out	shalach	שָׁלַח
Let my people go! (Ex. 7:16)	shalach et ami	שַׁלַּח אֶת עַמִּי
to launch a rocket	shilach **until**	שִׁלַּח טִיל
to set fire to, burn	shilach ba-esh	שִׁלַּח בָּאֵשׁ
to divorce one's wife	shilach et ishto	שִׁלַּח אֶת אִשְׁתּוֹ
and he sent (Gen. 32:3(4 תנ״ך)) (KAL form)	va-yishlach	וַיִּשְׁלַח
and so he will let go (Ex. 6:11) (PIEL form)	vishalach	וִישַׁלַּח

Hit the Trail!

Evil Lets Go

> " *After Pharaoh had let the people go, God did not guide them . . . through the land of the P'lishtim . . . God thought that the people, upon seeing war, might change their minds and return to Egypt.* "—Ex. 13:17

B 'SHALACH Par'oh (*When Pharaoh let go, finally*), God leads Yisra'el to freedom. The short route, a direct path by caravan along the Mediterranean coast to 'Aza (*Gaza*), takes eleven days.

God leads Yisra'el out with an upraised hand.

V'lo nacham Elohim (*But God did not lead*) them along the short route, pen yinachem (*lest they repent*) warfare and wish to return to Egypt (Ex. 13:17). In fact, later at Kadesh, Yisra'el will fear the report of the scouts and actually try to find a leader to guide them back to Egypt (Num. 14:4).

For this reason, God chooses the longer, windier, southern route toward the Yam Suf (*Sea of Reeds*), Chorev, and Sinai. The site of the burning bush is familiar territory for Moshe (Ex. 3:12). But Pharaoh will think that the desert bars the way. At Pi haChirot (*Mouth of Freedom*), Yisra'el goes out b'yad ramah (*with an upraised hand*), and God hardens Pharaoh's heart for one final time (Ex. 14:8).

? Read Ex. 13:15. The last time Pharaoh stubbornly refused "to let go," God killed Egyptian firstborns. This time the stage is set for judgment upon the hosts (army) of Egypt. Explain how Egypt pays the ransom for the army of Yisra'el.

The Army Pursues

> **❝** *The Egyptians went after them, all the horses and chariots of Pharaoh, with his cavalry and army, and overtook them as they were encamped by the sea, by Pi-Hachirot, in front of Ba'al-Tz'fon.* **❞**   —Ex. 14:9

Ba'al Tz'fon (*Lord of the North*) is the only Egyptian idol that God did not destroy [Ex. 12:12; Mekhilta; Rashi, Ibn Ezra]. God directs Yisra'el to encamp at Mouth of Freedom, facing Ba'al Tz'fon (Ex. 14:2).

Pharaoh repents letting go.

Pharaoh is deluded into thinking that Yisra'el is shut in by the wilderness (Ex. 14:3), and that Ba'al Tz'fon can take on God (Ex. 14:4). God hardens Pharaoh's heart, saying

v'ikavdah b'far'oh oov'chol-cheylo (*I will be glorified over Pharaoh and all his army*, Ex. 14:4).

It is 21 Nisan, the seventh day of Passover. Yisra'el looks up, v'hinei Mitzrayim nosea (*and behold Egypt marches*) as a single, unified force. Terror strikes Yisra'el: "Weren't there enough graves in Egypt?" (Ex. 14:10-11).

But Moshe turns away fear with a word of assurance: "Stop being so fearful! The LORD will make war for you, v'atem ta'harishun (*and you be still*)" (Ex. 14:13-14).

?
Pharaoh says, "I will pursue and overtake, divide the spoil and gorge myself" (Ex. 15:9). Read Ps. 50:3, and contrast with Ps. 50:21, Is. 42:14, and Ex. 15:13, 16. What moves God from silence to active redemption?

Part the Sea!

> ❝ ADONAI asked Moshe, "Why are you crying to
> me? Tell the people of Isra'el to go forward! Lift
> your staff, reach out with your hand over the sea,
> and divide it in two." ❞
> —Exodus 14:15-16a

ivine imperatives: Let them march forward! Hold your staff high! Extend your hand! Split the sea! Thus, the LORD responds to the threat of Egypt marching [Ex. 14:10; Fox, p. 352].

God orders Yisra'el to march across the deep.

The LORD's moment has come! He proclaims: Behold, I will make hard the heart of Egypt, v'ikavdah (*and I will be glorified*) through Pharaoh and all his army (Ex. 14:17).

That night, the pillar of fire shines on Yisra'el, and darkness engulfs Egypt (Ex. 14:20). The east winds blow, and a path through the deep opens for the children of Yisra'el (Ex. 14:21). At 2 a.m. [Rashi], the children of Yisra'el move across, faced by walls of water on either side (Ex. 14:22, 24a). Pharaoh and his hosts pursue, but the chariot wheels bog, and the sand becomes a quagmire with no escape. Egypt panics: I must flee from before Yisra'el! The LORD is fighting for them against Egypt! (Ex. 14:25).

❓ *Compare and contrast Ex. 14:17, 25. In an unusual word play, the Hebrew root "kaved" has a dual use. Here the wheels of the chariots are "made heavy" while the LORD "gains glory." Explain how the deep serves God's purposes.*

Drown the Army!

" *ADONAI said to Moshe, "Reach your hand out over the sea, and the water will return and cover the Egyptians with their chariots and cavalry."* "

—*Exodus 14:26*

Stunning parallel use of the divine command, "Reach your hand out over the sea," ties the Shlishi and the R'vi'i segments (Ex. 14:16a, 26).

> *One army falls, and another army is purchased.*

This time, the deep collapses upon the hosts of Pharaoh! The army is obliterated! "Not by force, and not by power, but by My Spirit," says ADONAI-Tzva'ot (*the LORD of Hosts*, Zech. 4:6). Va-yar Yisra'el et-ha-yad ha-g'dolah (*and Israel saw the great hand*)

of the LORD (Ex. 14:31), and they believed in God and in his servant Moshe.

An outburst of song follows: I will sing unto the LORD for He has triumphed gloriously, the horse and rider thrown into the sea (Ex. 15:1). The singing continues with Mi Chamocha (*Who is like You?*) (Ex. 15:11), for even the deep obeys His voice. There is much singing about the greatness of God's right hand (Ex. 15:6, 12). Finally, with the greatness of God's right arm, the firstborn Yisra'el is "purchased" (Ex. 15:16; cf. Ex. 4:22, Gen. 4:1).

? *Read Luke 8:22-25. Do you think the talmidim of Yeshua actually say, "Mi chamocha?" when Yeshua stills the raging seas? Reread Ex. 15:10-11. What is the response of the faithful to God's manifestations of signs and wonders?*

Living Water

> **" They came to Eilim, where there were twelve springs and seventy palms. "** — *Exodus 15:27*

E ilim (place of *terebinths*) is the first desert oasis of the wilderness experience. Located about ten miles south of Marah (place of *bitter waters*), Eilim portrays the honeymoon aspect of the wilderness experience (Jer. 2:2).

God responds favorably to Yisra'el's grumbling.

Here, one pictures the ideal oasis, with a spring for every tribe and a palm for every elder. The segment ends with the LORD responding favorably to the grumblings of the people and calling them to "come close, into the presence of ADONAI" (Ex. 16:9). Even as Aharon delivers God's message, the congregation beholds the glory of the LORD appearing in the clouds (Ex. 16:10).

Exactly a month after Yisra'el has left Sinai, supplies run short. The people grumble, "We wish ADONAI had used his own hand to kill us off in Egypt!" (Ex. 16:3). But God's response is to open the skies and to "cause bread to rain down from heaven" (Ex. 16:4).

Read Ex. 16:4 and Jn. 6:57-61, 66. In both instances, God tests whether or not his followers will walk in His Torah (instruction). Determine whether God is trying to salvage a bad honeymoon or showing patience for his bride.

Bread from Heaven

> **"** . . . *and* ADONAI *said to Moshe, "I have heard the grumblings of the people of Isra'el. Say to them: 'At dusk you will be eating meat, and in the morning you will have your fill of bread . . . '"* **"**   —Ex. 16:11-12

Providential care! God interrupts the natural order to establish the ideal relationship as it was b'Reisheet (*in the beginning*).

Man receives bread without toil, the manna that comes from heaven (Ex. 16:4, 14-15). An Egyptian word, "man" means *gift* or "*coming from the sky every day*" [Kaplan, p. 336].

> ### God tenderly cares for the needs of His people.

The miracle of manna, as the "bread of heaven," has been explained as a natural excretion of aphids in symbiosis with the tamarisk tree. These insects need to consume enormous amounts of sugary sap in order to get sufficient nitrogen for metabolism. Manna is a natural excretion of sugars [Bodenheimer, 1947].

The miracle is that the manna was found in such giant quantities that each person could gather an omer (5.1 pints, Ex. 16:16), that the manna could not be found on the Shabbat (Ex. 16:25-27), and that God lovingly fed His people with tender care for forty years (Ex. 16:35).

> ? Read Ex. 16:4-5, 26-30. The decalog commands that Yisra'el keep Shabbat holy; but Yisra'el hasn't reached Sinai and the commandments have not yet been given (Ex. 20: 8-11). Explain why God is teaching Shabbat rest.

Test and Be Tested

> ❝ *The whole community of the people of Isra'el left the Seen Desert, traveling in stages, as* ADONAI *had ordered, and camped at Refidim; but there was no water for the people to drink.* ❞ —Exodus 17:1

Murmuring has its limits. Moshe asks, "Why are you testing ADONAI?" (Ex. 17:2). The setting is R'fidim, two days' journey southeast of Eilim. Encampment locations at Dofkah and Alush (Num. 33:12-14) are omitted in the Exodus account to focus on incidents of murmuring [Hertz, p. 278].

Again, the lack of water becomes a stumbling stone. "The people quarreled with Moshe" (Ex. 17:2a). Moshe asks, "Mah-t'rivun imadi? Mah-t'nasun et-haShem? (*For what do you quarrel with me?*

For what do you test ADONAI?, Ex. 17:2b). Thus, the place is named Massah (*Testing*) and M'rivah (*Quarreling*, Ex. 17:7), because the people strove with God and tested Him.

The murmuring hardens into strife and contention.

The fruits of murmuring sow thorns for the future. Contention breeds contention. Strife at Massah is linked to the coming attack of Amalek [Sforno on Ex. 17:2, 8]. Now it is Yisra'el who will be tested!

? *Read Gen. 36:12 and Num 24:20. Amalek is the firstborn of Esav's firstborn, born to a Canaanite concubine who sought to intermarry. Explain how Amalek contends with Yisra'el for the status of firstborn among the nations.*

War with Evil

> **❝** *Moshe built an altar, called it* ADONAI *Nissi [*ADONAI *is my banner/miracle] and said, "Because their hand was against the throne of Yah,* ADONAI *will fight 'Amalek generation after generation."* **❞** —Ex. 17:15-16

Amalek's name must be completely eradicated. Otherwise, according to the oath of the LORD, the kes-YAH (abbreviation for *throne* of the *Holy One*) shall not be shalem (*whole*) [Rashi, Ex. 17:16; cf. Gen. 36: 40-43 in *Walk Genesis!*, p. 149].

> ### Amalek, the evil twin of Yisra'el, must die.

Indeed, the phrase, "the hand is on God's Throne," doubles for a divine oath, until Amalek is completely wiped out [Mekhilta].

Not just the existence, but the very memory of Amalek is targeted for obliteration. Targeted for utter destruction is the zekher-Amalek (a wordplay doubling for *males of Amalek* and *memory of Amalek*).

The oath is written as a zikaron (*memorial*) which is transmitted b'sefer (*into a book*) v'sim b'aznei Y'hoshua (*and put into the ears of Joshua*, Ex. 17:14).

This oath is so serious that Israel's first king, King Saul, will be stripped of his throne for failing to annihilate the cattle along with the king of Amalek (1 Sam. 15:14-28).

> **?** *Read Ex. 17:16 and 1 Sam. 15:32-33. God's oath is to destroy all Amalekites [Sanh. 20b]. Explain Sh'muel's words: "Just as your sword has left women childless, so will your mother be left childless among women."*

Destroy All Evil!   *Meander*

> ❝ *"May all your enemies perish like this, ADONAI; but may those who love him be like the sun going forth in its glory!" Then the land had rest for forty years.*❞
>
> Judges 5:31

Sisra, captain of the army of Canaanite King Yavin, oppressed Yisra'el for twenty years. Like Pharaoh, he had a huge force of iron chariots (Jd. 4:2-3). In both cases, the chariots bogged down while pursuing Yisra'el and the armies panic (Jd. 4:15, cf. Ex. 14:24-25).

Once again, the LORD gives marching orders, and the entire army is destroyed (Jd. 4:7,16; cf. Ex. 14:15, 28). What has changed this time is that the hosts of Yisra'el are fighting, and the battle is taking place inside the Land of Promise. When the Canaanites are routed, it is D'vorah and Barak who sing the song of rejoicing (Jd. 5).

Evil must be uprooted for a generation to find peace.

Curiously, the song ends with a vignette on Sisra's mother. She rationalizes, "Of course! They're collecting and dividing the spoil" (Jd. 5:28-30). She waits, wistfully confident and completely unaware that God has hardened Sisra, her Canaanite son, for final judgment (Jd. 4:9).

? *Read Judges 5:31. This verse concludes the longest Haftarah in the entire reading cycle. Explain the concluding words that "the land had rest for forty years." Relate long life to the sons of C'na'an and of Amalek.*

...ings   A Thousand-Year Peace!

❝ *Blessed and holy is anyone who has a part in the first resurrection; over him the second death has no power . . . they will be cohanim . . . and . . . rule with him for the thousand years.* ❞   —Revelation 20:6

"ADONAI, God of heaven's armies, has begun his reign!" (Rev. 19:6). The crowd continues, "For the time has come for the wedding of the Lamb, and His Bride . . ." (Rev. 19:7).

God establishes His throne for 1000 years.

The angel of God tells the birds of creation to prepare to gorge themselves on the flesh of kings, generals, important men, horses and riders from all the nations (Rev. 19:18).

Once more, God summons the forces of the deep to serve His purposes. The "lake of fire that burns with sulfur" engulfs the beast and false prophet, while the birds gorge on the slain armies that fought the LORD and His Hosts (Rev. 19:20-21). Satan himself along with all evil is chained and thrown into the Abyss for a thousand years (Rev. 20:2-3).

Martyrs and those who risked their lives now triumph over death. They rule with Messiah over all nations of earth in a peaceful theocracy lasting for a thousand years!

? • *Read Heb. 10:5-9, 7:23-25 and 1 Sam. 14:20-26. King Saul lost throne and dynasty, because he feared annihilating Amalek's throne. Discuss the throne that Messiah and His martyrs inherit, when God establishes his Throne.*

Talk Your Walk . . .

When Pharaoh finally lets go, the sons of Yisra'el are forcibly expelled from Egypt by the hand of Pharaoh himself! The sons of Yisra'el come out with upraised arms, glorying in the power of the LORD.

Pharaoh changes his mind and organizes his iron chariots to cut down the children of Yisra'el at Pi haChirot (*the Mouth of Freedom*). It is the 21st of Nisan, the seventh day of Passover. God orders Moshe to split the sea. The sons of Yisra'el march into the deep! Pharaoh follows; but Moshe is ordered to raise his arm once more, and the waters close in. Pharaoh's chariots are bogged down, and suddenly the hosts of Egypt are drowned in the surging waters of the deep. Yisra'el sings Mi Chamocha (*Who is like You*), worshipping God in song.

The nation has been purchased and now enters the destiny to walk with God through the wilderness into the Land of Promise.

> *Yisra'el is redeemed to eliminate evil.*

The wilderness experience begins like a honeymoon. God tenderly provides living water from desert oases and manna, the bread from heaven. But Yisra'el's complaints grow into strife and contention. For testing God, Yisra'el will be tested. In this spirit, Amalek challenges Yisra'el's chosen position. Esav's grandson by a concubine vies with Yisra'el for firstborn among nations; God declares war forever!

Oasis

. . . Walk Your Talk

Throughout the Torah scroll, the Hebrew flows poetically, until in Exodus an exceptionally wide column breaks the barriers separating one normal-sized column from another (Ex. 14:28-15:23). It is mesmerizing—almost as if the rules of grammar were suspended to make room for the movement of the deep across the page. All normalcy breaks apart as creation celebrates the redemption of God's firstborn. Shirat haYam (*the Song of the Sea*) is still sung today, and the congregation rises as this song is chanted.

Rites of passage are those critical experiences which initiate us into adulthood. For the children of Yisra'el, redemption meant deliverance from the dangers of warfare and the deep. "Yea, though I walk through

> *Those who walk with God grow into sonship.*

the valley of the shadow of death, I will fear no evil, for thou art with me; thy rod and thy staff they comfort me" (Ps. 23:4, KJV).

Circumcision, bar mitzvah, weddings, apprenticeships, and yes, signing mortgage contracts—with each experience, we grow a bit older and wiser. Are you walking in faith with God through the deep places? Are you risking your life to walk with Him?

Shabbat Shalom!

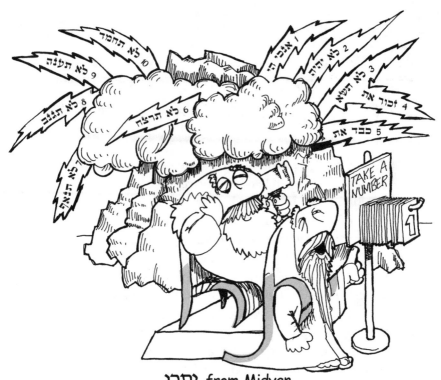

יתרו, from Midyan,
Moshe's father-in-law,
listened to
the Exodus story in awe.
This priest gave advice
as a wise old pa:
"Delegate to judges!
Stop being the Law!"

Moshe climbed high up
onto Sinai's peak.
The mountain quaked,
and the people did freak!
Then down came God—
He wanted to speak
as the "Father-In-Law"
of those who seek.

Walk YITRO!
18:1-20:26(23 תָּנִ"ךְ)

Jethro (abundance)

TORAH—Exodus 18:1-20:26(23 תָּנִ"ךְ)
- 1st Yitro Worships—Exodus 18:1
- 2nd Yitro Advises—Exodus 18:13
- 3rd Judges Appointed—Exodus 18:24-25a
- 4th Destination Sinai—Exodus 19:1
- 5th The Prophetic Calling—Exodus 19:7
- 6th Adoption of the Nation—Exodus 19:20
- 7th Seeing and Trembling—Exodus 20:18(15 תָּנִ"ךְ)
- Maftir Approaching God—Exodus 20:26(23 תָּנִ"ךְ)

HAFTARAH—Isaiah 6:1-7:6; 9:6-7(5-6 תָּנִ"ךְ)
- Divine Rule—Isaiah 9:7(6 תָּנִ"ךְ)

B'RIT CHADASHAH—Matthew 5:8-20
- Keep My Commandments—Matthew 5:20

Instruction from Our "Fathers-In-Law"

← Looking Back

B'REISHEET (*in the beginning*), God commands man to be fruitful, multiply, fill the earth, and subdue it. Man disobeys, choosing destruction, exile, and death. God purposes to redeem mankind, and Chanoch, Noach, and Avraham all walk with God. Promises of a nation to bless the nations of the world take shape through Avraham's growing family, still struggling but reunited in Egypt.

Exodus begins: These are the SH'MOT (*names*) of Ya'akov's royal family, chosen by God. He blesses them, as before the fall, to be fruitful. The nation-in-embryo multiplies exceedingly, fills the land of Goshen, and threatens the empire of Egypt. To halt the growth, Pharaoh oppresses the sons of Yisra'el, fulfilling God's prophecy more than four hundred years before.

VA'ERA (*and I appeared*), says the LORD, to make good on My promises to Avraham to redeem the nation. God tells Moshe, **BO** (*enter!*) and make final negotiations with Pharaoh to free the sons of Yisra'el. Measure for measure, God punishes Pharaoh.

> These are the SH'MOT *of sons,*
> *suffering down in Egypt.*
> *God remembers us:*
> VA'ERA *to keep My promises.*
> *Now* BO, *negotiate to*
> *let My people go!*
> B'SHALACH *Pharaoh,*
> *God leads us through the sea.*
> YITRO *rejoices*
> *to hear of God's mighty deeds!*

B'SHALACH Par'oh (*when Pharaoh let go*), God personally leads Yisra'el. The sons of Yisra'el go out of Egypt with hands upraised, a symbol of their redemption from slavery and oppression. Pharaoh, hardened one last time, gives

Log

chase to re-enslave the redeemed. A week after Passover, Yisra'el sees Egypt marching as one man! God orders Moshe to split the sea! Egypt is hardened. The army follows Yisra'el, walking upon the deep of the parted sea bed. The waters close, and the deep swallows the entire army! Yisra'el sees and believes in the LORD and in Moshe. It is the high point of trust—the climax of the signs and wonders. Despite the nation's grumbling, God personally guides them to a gorgeous oasis at Eilim. He feeds the nation mannah from heaven. The picture of 70 elders and 70 palm trees is idyllic.

YITRO (*Jethro/abundance*), Moshe's father-in-law, hears about the signs and wonders

In YITRO . . .

The Key People are Yitro (*Jethro*), Moshe (*Moses*), Tsiporah (*Zipporah*), Gershom, El'azar (*Eleazer*), and Aharon (*Aaron*).

The Scenes include the wilderness of Sinai and Mt. Sinai.

Main Events include Yitro hearing what God has done, rejoicing, and giving Moshe advice to delegate part of his duties as judge; the LORD coming down on Mt. Sinai and speaking the Ten Commandments, the people trembling, and Moshe approaching God alone.

God has done. He comes to Moshe. They worship God with offerings and celebrate a covenant meal with the nation's leaders at the foot of Mount Sinai . . .

The Trail Ahead

Compass

The Path

וַיִּשְׁמַע יִתְרוֹ כֹהֵן מִדְיָן חֹתֵן מֹשֶׁה
אֵת כָּל אֲשֶׁר עָשָׂה אֱלֹהִים
לְמֹשֶׁה וּלְיִשְׂרָאֵל עַמּוֹ
כִּי הוֹצִיא יְהוָה
אֶת יִשְׂרָאֵל מִמִּצְרַיִם

—שְׁמוֹת יח/א

letter:	vav	reish	tav	yod
	וֹ	ר	תָּ	יְ
sound:	Oh	R	T	Yee

Jethro (abundance) = YITRO = **יתרו**

Work

and heard Jethro	*va-yish'ma Yitro*	וַיִּשְׁמַע יִתְרוֹ
priest of Midian	*cohen Midyan*	כֹּהֵן מִדְיָן
father-in-law of Moses	*choten Mosheh*	חֹתֵן מֹשֶׁה
— all that	*et kol-asher*	אֵת כָּל־אֲשֶׁר
did God	*asah Elohim*	עָשָׂה אֱלֹהִים
for Moses	*l'Mosheh*	לְמֹשֶׁה
and for Israel people-His	*oo-l'Yisra'el amo*	וּלְיִשְׂרָאֵל עַמּוֹ
that brought out the LORD	*ki hotsi ADONAI*	כִּי־הוֹצִיא יְהֹוָה
— Israel	*et-Yisra'el*	אֶת־יִשְׂרָאֵל
from Egypt	*mi-Mitsrayim*	מִמִּצְרָיִם׃

—Exodus 18:1

Related Words

abundance, remainder	*yeter*	יֶתֶר
advantage, superiority, profit, gain	*yitrone*	יִתְרוֹן
spiritual elation (additional soul)	*n'shamah y'terah*	נְשָׁמָה יְתֵרָה
to add, overdo, exaggerate	*yiter*	יִתֵּר
superfluous	*m'yootar*	מְיֻתָּר
more than	*yoter*	יוֹתֵר
too much (more than enough)	*yoter mi-dai*	יוֹתֵר מִדַּי

Hit the Trail!

Yitro Worships

❝ *Now Yitro the priest of Midyan, Moshe's father-in-law, heard about all that God had done for Moshe and for Isra'el his people, how* ADONAI *had brought Isra'el out of Egypt.* ❞ —*Exodus 18:1*

Yitro journeys to reunite with Moshe, and he brings Moshe's wife and children to Har-haElohim (*the mountain of God*, Ex. 18:5). Parallels with the reunion of Ya'akov and his family abound (Gen. 37:1-2; 47:27-28).

Moshe meets Yitro near Sinai [Ramban]. Excitement builds, on the brink of God's confirmation of promises made at the burning bush to worship God on this very mountain (Ex. 3:1, 12).

Yitro marvels that God split the sea and warred with Amalek. Va-yichad Yitro (*and Jethro prickled*), either with joy [Or haChaim in Stone, p. 396] or unease [Rashi, 1995, p. 210]. Yitro is thrilled that God paid back Pharaoh, measure for measure (Ex. 18:9-11).

Yitro eats a covenant meal with God as Elohim.

Yitro worships God by bringing an olah (*ascent offering*) and offering z'vachim (*offerings*) at a covenant meal, which he eats near the mount with Aharon and the elders of Yisra'el (Ex. 18:12; Gen. 8:20).

? *Read Ex. 18:12 and Luke 22:25-27. Rashi comments that Moshe's name is not mentioned at the covenant feast because he served the guests. Discuss servant leadership in the context of traditional Jewish understandings.*

Yitro Advises

> **"** *The following day Moshe sat to settle disputes for the people, while the people stood around Moshe from morning till evening.* **"**
>
> —*Exodus 18:13*

Moshe is overwhelmed, arbitrating disputes and sitting as judge "from morning till evening" (Ex. 18:13). Yitro observes that Moshe "sits alone" while the people stand around (Ex. 18:14).

Yitro advises Moshe that the people can help judge.

He tells Moshe: "it's not good," "you'll wear out," "it's kaved (*too heavy*)," and "you can't do it alone" (Ex. 18:17-18; cf. Ex. 17:12). Then Yitro offers advice that begins with the identical expression the LORD spoke to Avraham while he was on the mount with Yitzchak: Sh'ma b'koli (*Listen to my voice!*, Ex. 18:19; cf. Gen. 22:18). "I will advise you, so that God may be-there with you" [Ex. 18:19, Fox].

Moshe must lead by example: et-ha-derech yelchu vahh (*the way, they must walk in it*, Ex. 18:20). Moshe must also delegate authority to judges—able men who fear God, truthful men who do not take bribes. These men will share the burden, v'tsiv'cha Elohim (*and God command you so!*, Ex. 18:23).

? **Read Ex. 18:22.** *The judges are to decide small matters and bring the great matters to Moshe (e.g., decisions of case law). In so doing, the burden upon Moshe is made light. How does this impact your understanding of Mt. 11:30?*

Judges Appointed

Moshe paid attention to his father-in-law's counsel and did everything he said. Moshe chose competent men from all Isra'el and made them heads over the people . . . ❞ —*Exodus 18:24-25a*

Advice implemented! Moshe appoints judges, anshei-chayil (*men capable*) of high caliber and exemplary character, to administer over the thousands, hundreds, fifties, and tens (Ex. 18:25).

Judiciary is implemented en route to nationhood.

The judiciary is set up with an appeal system. More difficult matters are sent up the chain, and only the most difficult of matters reach Moshe for rulings. Thus, Moshe can devote himself fully to Torah (godly *instruction*), without having his energies sapped on everyday affairs that others could easily handle instead.

Moshe bids farewell to Yitro. Va-y'shalach Moshe et-chot'no (*And Moshe lets go of his father-in-law*), who journeys back to his land (Ex. 18:27).

Thus, the judiciary is established. The system is implemented on the road to nationhood, and it is set in place immediately before the LORD reveals Himself to the people as a whole, at Sinai.

? *Terach, Avraham's father, remained in Charan (the crossroads). He did not go on to the Mount of the LORD. Yitro comes, but Moshe must reluctantly let him go back. Fathers die in the wilderness, but sons journey on. Comment.*

Destination Sinai

> **" In the third month after the people of Isra'el had left the land of Egypt, the same day they came to the Sinai Desert. "**
>
> —*Exodus 19:1*

What the LORD told Avram (Gen. 15:13) and Moshe (Ex. 3:12) now comes to pass. The moment begins with a break in the narrative structure.

Ba-chodesh ha-shlishi (*in the third month*) signals the start of a new narrative. The utter newness of it all breaks continuity with the last verse in the prior segment [Fox, p. 364]. It is the first day of Sivan, the day of the new moon [Shabb. 86b, Rashi]. The people leave R'fidim (Ex. 17:1, 8) and encamp opposite the mount of the LORD (Ex. 19:2).

God calls; Moshe ascends. It is morning of the second day. Moshe is commissioned by God as prophet, the ear of the people to God, and the mouth of God to the people.

God calls Yisra'el as His treasured, chosen people.

"Tishm'u b'koli (*listen to My voice*)" is the crucial idea. Says the LORD, "Im shamo'a tishm'u b'koli (*if you listen diligently to My voice*) and keep My covenant, then you will be to Me a s'gulah (*treasure*) from among all peoples" (Ex. 19:5).

Look up verses with "s'gulah" (Ex. 19:5; 1 Chr. 29:8; Eccl. 2:8) and "am s'gulah" (Dt. 7:6, 14:2, 26:18). Compare these verses to 1 Pet. 2:9: "a chosen people, the King's cohanim, a holy nation, and a people for God to possess!"

The Prophetic Calling

" *Moshe came, summoned the leaders of the people and presented them with all these words which ADONAI had ordered him to say.* "

—*Exodus 19:7*

The exact location of Sinai and the exact time when the LORD speaks to the people at Mount Sinai are shrouded in the mists of the unknown. A most ancient second century midrashic source, the Mekhilta, says the LORD spoke to the people on the sixth of Sivan, on a Friday.

Prepare three days, for the LORD shall speak!

Moshe knows he will worship the LORD at Sinai, because the LORD had told him many years ago (Ex. 3:12). On the new moon, the people arrive; early the next morning, Moshe goes up. On 2 Sivan, God commissions Moshe as prophet and calls the people to serve him (Ex. 19:6). Moshe returns, summons the leaders, and the people agree (Ex.19:7-8). Early the next morning, Moshe goes up again.

The LORD tells Moshe that the people will personally hear Him speak to Moshe, so that they will believe—forever —in the LORD and in His prophet (Ex. 19:9; cf. 14:31). Three days later, God and Moshe speak! (Ex. 19:9b, 19).

Read Ex. 19:9-11. R. Yose thinks that the people cleanse themselves and prepare for three full days [Shabb. 87a].
Rashi and the Mekhilta say the people prepare 4-5 Sivan until Friday, 6 Sivan, the third day. What do you think?

Adoption of the Nation

> ❝ ADONAI *came down onto Mount Sinai, to the top of the mountain; then* ADONAI *called Moshe to the top of the mountain; and Moshe went up.* ❞
>
> —*Exodus 19:20*

Heavenly clouds descend upon Sinai [Dt. 4:36; Ps. 18:9 (10 תנ״ך); Mekhilta]. The nation is ritually pure, having washed clothes, cleansed at mikveh, and abstained from sexual relations for three days [Ex. 19:14-15; Lev. 15:16-18; Shabb. 86a; Durham, p. 265]. Moshe is called to the top (Ex. 19:20)!

The LORD speaks personally to His people.

More detail of these events is recorded in the next parashah (esp. Ex. 24:15-18). Quite simply, the LORD speaks.

The decalog in stone is not given at this time. What is spotlighted is the LORD speaking directly to His people.

As with the location and time, so the manner of God's speaking remains mysterious. Some say that the Ten Words were spoken together and instantaneously [Makk. 24a]. Some say that all Ten Words were first spoken together. Then the first two commands were repeated; but the people freaked, pleading that God speak only to Moshe [Rashi, Ramban, Ex. 20:16, Dt. 5:25(22 תנ״ך)].

❓ *Read Aseret haDibrot (the Ten Words) in Ex. 20:1-14.*
Note the Ten Words are spoken as very broad principles.
● *There are no rules for enforcing violations of the principles. Explain why the legal parts are not spoken at this time.*

Seeing and Trembling

> **"** *All the people experienced the thunder, the lightning, the sound of the shofar, and the mountain smoking. When the people saw it, they trembled . . .* **"**
> —*Exodus 20:18 (15 תנ״ך)*

Impossible as it may seem, Jewish tradition claims that the people actually "saw" thunder. "V'chol ha'am ro'im et ha-kolot (*and all the people seeing voices/ thunder*)" describes this mindbending experience (Ex. 20:18 (15 תנ״ך)). Bullinger [p. 135] calls this "seeing" a zeugma, a rhetorical figure in which a verb has two objects ("the people saw lightning, [heard] thunder").

Yisra'el works out her salvation in fear and trembling. They beg Moshe, "You, speak with us . . . But don't let God speak with us, or we will die" (Ex. 20:19 (16 תנ״ך)).

Moshe answers, "Don't be afraid, because God has come only to test you and make you fear him" (Ex. 20:20(17 תנ״ך)). At Massah, the people tested God, but now God tests them.

The LORD elevates Yisra'el and Moshe, His prophet.

The people respond by showing faith in God and in Moshe as His prophet. They watch from outside the bounds around the mount. Then, nigash Moshe (*Moses drew near*) "to the thick darkness where God was" (Ex. 20:21(18 תנ״ך)).

? *Yisra'el is elevated to the status of being chosen to draw near to the LORD. Yet at the moment of exaltation, the people are feeling unholy and fearing for their lives. Explain how you are preparing to hear God's voice.*

Approaching God

> ❝ Likewise, you are not to use steps to go up to my altar; so that you won't be indecently uncovered. ❞
> —*Exodus 20:26 (23 תנ״ך)*

The maftir summarizes ADONAI's words, spoken directly to the people: "You yourselves have seen that I spoke with you from heaven" (Ex. 20:22 (19 תנ״ך)). After hearing the second command (Ex. 20:23 (20 תנ״ך)), the people believed in God and in Moshe as prophet.

Torah is God's instruction on how to approach Him.

From inside the cloud, the LORD tells Moshe that He will come not just to Sinai, but every place His people build altars and offer olot and z'vachim (*ascent and sacrificial offerings*, Ex. 20:24 (21 תנ״ך)). Such altars are to be made of stone, not profaned by weapons of war (Ex. 20:25(22 תנ״ך)). These altars differ from the copper altar of the tabernacle [Childs, p. 466]. Priests ascend by ramp, not unlike the ramp in Ya'akov's dream at Beit-El (Ex. 20:26(23 תנ״ך); Gen. 28:12).

In congregations today, one ascends the bimah to read Torah and hear the Word of God. The service captures the moment when man ascends to God's abode to meet with Him and receive Torah.

? Read Gen. 28:12. At Beit-El, Ya'akov dreams of a ramp connecting heaven and the land [Hamilton, p. 239; Alter, 1981, p. 149; cf. Gen. 11:4]. Discuss the spiritual idea that God invites everyone to walk from earth into His Presence.

Divine Rule   *Meander*

> **" in order to extend the dominion and perpetuate the peace of the throne and kingdom of David, . . . henceforth and forever. The zeal of ADONAI-Tzva'ot will accomplish this. "** —Isaiah 9:7 (6 תנ"ך)

At his commissioning, the prophet Y'sha'yahu (*Isaiah*) sees a vision of the LORD sitting upon His throne (Is. 6:1).

God establishes His throne.

The house is "filled with smoke," the s'rafim (*guardian angels*) are singing 'Holy, holy, holy!', and the doorposts shake "at the sound of their shouting" (Is. 6:2-4). Y'sha'yahu hears the voice of God and says, "Send me!" (Is. 6:8-9).

But the people are being hardened for judgment. The kings of Syria and Yisra'el conspire against Achaz, king of Y'hudah, to remove him and install ben Tav'el (*the son of Tabeel*) as a puppet government (Is. 7:6).

Y'sha'yahu takes his son, Sh'ar Yashuv (*A Remnant Will Return*), and tells Achaz to stay calm and not fear (Is. 7:4). The Haftarah then skips ahead two chapters to announce that the zeal of ADONAI-Tz'vaot (*the LORD of Hosts*) will guarantee the Davidic throne. Messiah will come (Is. 9:6-7(5-6 תנ"ך))!!!

? Read Is. 9:7(6תנ"ך): "to the <u>increase</u> of His rulership and to completeness, there will be no end." Curiously, the Hebrew for <u>increase</u> begins with a mem sofeet. Why is shalom/peace/wholeness still in the future?

...*ings* Keep My Commandments

> **"** *For I tell you that unless your righteousness is far greater than that of the Torah-teachers and P'rushim, you will certainly not enter the Kingdom of Heaven!* **"**
>
> —*Matthew 5:20*

Some think it silly that the LORD could talk to Yisra'el from a mountain top at Sinai. Here, Yeshua speaks His famous Sermon on the Mount.

> ### God in heaven meets man on the mount.

Various groups receive favor from God: "How blessed are the pure in heart! for they will see God" (Mt. 5:8). Yet David has already written, "The earth is ADONAI's . . . Who may go up to the mountain of the ADONAI? . . . Those with clean hands and pure hearts" (Ps. 24:1-4).

Another favored group, the peacemakers, will be called sons of God (Mt. 5:9). Messiah, the promised Son to sit on David's throne, is named Sar Shalom (*Prince of Peace*, Is. 9:6(5 תנ"ך)).

In the Sermon on the Mount, the LORD extends His offer made at Sinai. The righteous and holy may draw near to God. They are permitted even to enter the Kingdom of Heaven. But standards are extremely high. Their righteousness must surpass that of the Torah-teachers!

> **?** *Read Mt. 5:19. Why does Yeshua say, "Whoever disobeys the least of these mitzvot and teaches others to do so will be called the least in the Kingdom of Heaven?" Explain Kefa's words (Ac. 15:10), in light of Yeshua's teaching.*

Talk Your Walk . . .

The Mekhilta summarizes our acceptance of the LORD in the context of a covenant agreement:

"And God spoke all these words, saying, "I am the LORD your God, who brought you out of the land of Egypt, out of the house of bondage." How come the Ten Commandments were not stated at the very beginning of the Torah? The matter may be compared to the case of a king who came into a city. He said to the people, "May I rule over you?" They said to him, "Have you done us any good, that you should rule over us?" What did he then do? He built a wall for them, brought water for them, fought their battles. Then he said to them, "May I rule over you?" They said to him, "Yes, indeed." So the Omnipresent brought the Israelites out of Egypt, divided the sea for them, brought manna down for them, brought up the well for them, provided the quail for them, made war for them against Amalek. Then he said to them, "May I rule over you?" They said to him, "Yes, indeed . . . . For when all of them stood before Mount Sinai to receive the Torah, they were unanimous in receiving the dominion of God with a whole heart."

[Mekhilta, Bachodesh 5, p. 66]

> **God covenants with His people.**

The people stand as one collective person, seeing and trembling greatly! Thunder sounds and flashing torches fill the sky. A shofar blast grows louder and louder as the mountain smokes. Moshe rushes back to warn the people. Then, a thick silence, amazing tranquillity, the awesome stillness, and . . . God speaks the immortal—Aseret haDibrot (*The Ten Words*).

Oasis

... Walk Your Talk

Vicarious participation in history means more than an imaginary idea. When the children of Yisra'el stood at Mount Sinai, the fathers said, "Na'aseh v'nishma (*We will do and we will listen*)." Every Jewish person stood there, in the loins of the fathers. Just as the death of Yitzchak would have ended all subsequent Jewish life to come, so the decision of the fathers at Sinai bound all future generations to a life in covenant with the LORD. How many Germans, removed from Jewishness to the third and fourth generation, went to the camps screaming in German, "I'm not Jewish!" Was their participation in history as Jews—at the cost of their lives—vicarious, real, . . . or both?

At Sinai, the LORD spoke at least two commands that everyone heard: "Anochi ADONAI Eloheicha (*I Am the LORD, your God*)," and "You are to have no other gods before me" (Ex. 20:2-3).

> **To live the covenant, we must put God first.**

God commands first place. No other god—no one else but Him—is to occupy that circle! Are you possessive of God? Are you jealous for God's sake?

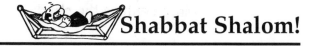 **Shabbat Shalom!**

In משפטים,
God told us, "Obey!"
Make wise <u>judgments</u>
to live His way!
Slaves work for six years,
then send 'em away!
Don't take a life,
or with *your* life, you'll pay!

Your judges must vote
their consciences true
and rule with fairness,
not just for the few.
"Na'aseh v'nishma!"
we all cry aloud.
Then up Sinai's peak,
Moshe enters the cloud.

Walk MISHPATIM!
21:1-24:18

Judgments

TORAH—Exodus 21:1-24:18
- 1st Liberty—Exodus 21:1-2
- 2nd Measure for Measure—Exodus 21:20
- 3rd Restitution—Exodus 22:5(4 תל"ך)
- 4th Authority—Exodus 22:28(27 תל"ך)
- 5th Impartiality—Exodus 23:6
- 6th Servanthood—Exodus 23:20
- 7th Prosperity —Exodus 23:26
- Maftir Entering God's Glory—Exodus 24:18

HAFTARAH—Jeremiah 34:8-22; 33:25-26
- Reaffirming Covenant—Jeremiah 33:25-26

B'RIT CHADASHAH—Matthew 17:1-13
- Re-entering God's Glory—Matthew 17:11-13

---

*Judgments for Governing
a Covenant Community*

Hiker's

◀ Looking Back

B'REISHEET (*in the beginning*), God commands man to be fruitful, multiply, fill the earth, and subdue it. Man disobeys, choosing destruction, exile, and death. God covenants to redeem mankind through those who walk with Him. Chanoch is raptured alive; Noach and his household float on the deep, saved by grace while all life is judged. Avraham is promised offspring to bless all families of the world.

Exodus begins: And these are the SH'MOT (*names*) of Ya'akov's sons, the royal family, chosen by God. The family in exile multiplies, fulfilling the pre-fall command to be fruitful. Pharaoh is threatened; he oppresses the sons of Yisra'el to stop the growth. VA'ERA (*and I appeared*), says the LORD, to verify My promises to Avraham and redeem his offspring from slavery in Egypt.

These are the SH'MOT of Ya'akov's sons, enslaved in Egypt. God says, VA'ERA to keep My promises. Now BO, negotiate to let My people go! B'SHALACH Pharaoh, we exit through the parted sea! YITRO advises Moshe to appoint judges who will govern by God's wise MISHPATIM.

God tells Moshe, **BO** (*enter!*) and negotiate to free the sons of Yisra'el. Measure for measure, God punishes Pharaoh. **B'SHALACH** Par'oh (*when Pharaoh let go*), God personally leads Yisra'el. The sons of Yisra'el exit with hands upraised, a symbol of their redemption from slavery and oppression. Pharaoh, hardened one last time, gives chase to re-enslave the redeemed. God orders Moshe to split the sea! Egypt is hard-

Log

ened. The army follows Yisra'el, walking on the deep of the parted sea. Waters close, and the deep swallows the army! Yisra'el believes in the LORD and Moshe. Then, on to Sinai!

YITRO (*Jethro/abundance*), Moshe's father-in-law, hears about the signs and wonders God has done. He comes and worships God with offerings. Watching Moshe judge all the next day, Yitro advises him to appoint a judiciary and to decide only the toughest cases himself. Judges are appointed, and Yitro returns home. For three days, the people wash and purify themselves to hear from the LORD. On Shavuot, God speaks the Ten Words! People are terrified! God calls Moshe to ascend to the summit.

In MISHPATIM . . .

The Key People are Moshe (*Moses*), Aharon (*Aaron*), Nadav (*Nadab*), Avihu (*Abihu*), the people of Yisra'el (*Israel*), 70 elders, Y'hoshua (*Joshua*), and Hur.

The Scene is Har Sinai (*Mt. Sinai*).

Main Events include rules about servants, property, resting, and keeping the three annual feasts; an angel sent to lead Yisra'el, go into C'na'an, and drive out the enemies; Moshe telling the LORD's judgments, the response, "Na'aseh v'nishma (*we will do and we will listen*);" Moshe sprinkling people with blood of the covenant; Moshe going up mountain to receive the tablets, staying 40 days and nights, and the glory of the LORD like fire.

There, the LORD speaks words which Moshe writes—Sefer haB'rit (*Book of the Covenant*), instruction for making wise **MISHPATIM** (*judgments*) . . .

The Trail Ahead ⮕

Compass

The Path

וְאֵלֶּה הַמִּשְׁפָּטִים
אֲשֶׁר תָּשִׂים לִפְנֵיהֶם
כִּי תִקְנֶה עֶבֶד עִבְרִי
שֵׁשׁ שָׁנִים יַעֲבֹד
וּבַשְּׁבִעִת יֵצֵא לַחָפְשִׁי חִנָּם

—שמות כא/א-ב

ם	י	ט	פָ	שׁ	מְ
letter:	mem sofeet	yod	tet	pay	shin	mem
sound:	M	EE	**Tee**	Pah	SH	Mee

judgments = **MISHPATIM** = מִשְׁפָּטִים

Work

& these the <u>judgments</u>	v'eleh ha-<u>mishpatim</u>	וְאֵלֶּה הַמִּשְׁפָּטִים
that you will put	asher tasim	אֲשֶׁר תָּשִׂים
before them	lif'neihem	לִפְנֵיהֶם:
if you buy	ki tikneh	כִּי תִקְנֶה
slave Hebrew	eved ivri	עֶבֶד עִבְרִי
six years he will work	shesh shanim ya'avod	שֵׁשׁ שָׁנִים יַעֲבֹד
and on the seventh	oo-va-sh'vi'it	וּבַשְּׁבִעִת
go out to freedom	yetse la-chofshi	יֵצֵא לַחָפְשִׁי
without paying	chinam	חִנָּם:

—Exodus 21:1-2

Related Words

justice, judgment, law, case, sentence	mishpaht	מִשְׁפָּט
judgment, punishment	shehfet	שֶׁפֶט
judge, judges	shofet, shof'tim	שׁוֹפֵט, שֹׁפְטִים
precedence (sentence of the firstling)	mishpaht ha-b'khorah	מִשְׁפַּט הַבְּכוֹרָה
death sentence	mishpaht mavet	מִשְׁפַּט מָוֶת
law court, court of justice (see also below)	beit-mishpaht	בֵּית־מִשְׁפָּט
law court, court of justice	beit-din	בֵּית־דִּין
jurist	mishp'tahn	מִשְׁפְּטָן

Hit the Trail!

Liberty

> **"** *These are the rulings you are to present to them: If you purchase a Hebrew slave, he is to work six years; but in the seventh, he is to be given his freedom without having to pay anything.* **"** —Exodus 21:1-2

Sefer haB'rit (*The Book of the Covenant*, Ex. 21:1-23:19) spells out ways to arrive at mishpatim (*rulings*). The parashah begins: "V'eleh ha-mishpatim asher tasim lifneihem (*And these are the rulings you are to set before them*)."

Rulings enforce principles of the Ten Words.

Sefer haB'rit is not really a law code of commandments to be observed. Rather, it is a guide for writing rulings to add enforcement provisions to the principles of Aseret haDibrot (*the Ten Words*).

Sefer haB'rit is "set before" the people—not "commanded" or "spoken" (Ex. 21:1). Civil rulings evolve into an enforceable code of law, from decisions based on case law.

The first ruling enforces the first principle that God freed Hebrew slaves. The court rules that Hebrew slaves must be set free after seven years. Any slave choosing to stay with his master must submit to having his ears pierced at the doorpost, thus negating his freedom [Stone, p. 418]. In any event, freedom is mandated at Jubilee [Lev. 25:54-55; Mish. Kidd. 1:2, Kidd. 22b].

> **?** *Read Ex. 21:2-6. "The ear heard My voice on Mt. Sinai ... And yet, this person has ... bought a master ... Therefore, let [his ear] be pierced" [Kidd. 22b]. Contrast doorpost use: for freedom at Passover, for slavery when ear piercing.*

Measure for Measure

❝ *If a person beats his male or female slave with a stick so severely that he dies, he is to be punished ...* ❞

—*Exodus 21:20*

Eye for eye and tooth for tooth—enacted literally—would have made Yisra'el a blind and toothless society. Rather, an abstract legal formula meaning "fair compensation" is stated as a ruling derived from case law.

Measure for measure means fair compensation.

The rishon segment dealt with the case of freeing Hebrew slaves. Talmud [Kidd. 14] says these were thieves who had been sold by the court to make restitution for debts they couldn't pay.

In this case (Ex. 21:20), the treatment of heathen slaves is discussed [Hertz, p. 308]. The ruling changes with the outcomes. If the slave dies that day, the master is punished [executed according to the Samaritan text, and Talmud, Sanh. 52b, Rashi]. If the slave dies later, the master has lost "his money" (Ex. 21:21). It may seem shocking that heathen slaves are treated as property. But the ruling states that a master suffers financial loss for an <u>unintended</u> result—discipline with a rod backfired.

? *Read Philemon 15-19. The broader question of freeing heathen slaves is bound up with Yisra'el's national calling. Yisra'el is the first nation to be freed from slavery. What are Rav Sha'ul's teachings concerning heathen slaves?*

Restitution

> " *If a person causes a field or vineyard to be grazed over or lets his animal loose to graze in someone else's field, he is to make restitution from the best produce of his own field . . .* " —*Exodus 22:5 (4* ך"נת*)*

Shen v'ayin (*tooth and eye*) damages are addressed. Here, cattle have grazed on an adjacent lot, doing damage to the field of the owner. Everyone knows that straying animals graze and trample!

Economic remedy must accompany all apologies.

The outcome should have been anticipated; so the ruling treats the situation as if the owner of the animals had been forewarned [Bav. Kam. 1-3; Gittin 85].

Restitution is always required for wrongs committed. It is never enough to ask for forgiveness and then move on. Here, the damages may have arisen from unintentional harm (such as the animal trampling crops under foot or engaging in excess grazing, leaving the ground barren in spots).

Torah mandates that the owner of the offending animal pay back not only measure for measure, but from the very choicest of his fields. Thus, a remedy is required for "pain and hassle" in addition to the damage caused.

? Read Mt. 18:8-9. Yeshua says, "And if your eye is a snare for you, gouge it out and fling it away!" Relate this to Ex. 21:23-27 and to the abstract idea of giving one's life in order to be set free from the death that is everlasting.

Authority

> **" You are not to curse God, and you are not to curse a leader of your people. "**
>
> —*Exodus 22:28 (27 תנ״ך)*

oly behavior should characterize attitudes toward authority figures, whether to Elohim (*God, the judge*) or to a nasi (*leader*). In Exodus 22:28 (27 תנ״ך), the command <u>lo t'kalel</u> (*do not honor lightly*), contrasts with <u>kaved,</u> (to *glorify, make heavy*).

> ### The rights of the needy always take precedence.

Phillippsohn [in Hertz, p. 315] relates this case to the previous segment (Ex. 22:27 (26 תנ״ך). God hears the cry of society's downtrodden. The judge must show compassion (even if a creditor has a legitimate right to keep a poor man's coat as collateral).

In Ex. 22:28 (27 תנ״ך), the judge's job makes him vulnerable to the curses of those whom he rules against. But the ruling goes further. Even if the ruler has erred and miscarried justice, he is not to be cursed. Feelings for humanity must always outweigh feelings of personal antipathy. The creditor is exhorted to remember, lo t'kalel (*do not curse* or *honor lightly*) those who are in authority.

? *Read Ex. 23:1-5, which addresses holiness in relationship to the wicked, the majority, the poor, and the enemy.*
• *Identify ways in which those in authority are to avoid natural human biases when rendering judgments.*

Impartiality

❝ *Do not deny anyone justice in his lawsuit simply because he is poor.* ❞

—*Exodus 23:6*

Oppression of the poor (needy) is denounced strongly! Judicial policy stresses protection of the innocent. If a high standard of proof is necessary to keep the innocent and righteous from being unfairly convicted, then the bar must be raised.

The judiciary must ensure justice for society's needy.

A high standard of proof may allow some of the wicked to escape judgment. Human error guarantees that some wicked will escape, and others who are innocent will not get justice in the courts. In practice, tradeoffs are necessary. However, the LORD sees everything! He promises to repay the wicked who escape judgment from the court (Ex. 23:7).

The emphasis upon protecting the poor and upon impartiality is designed to impress upon the society its founding principle, "I am ADONAI your God, who brought you out of the land of Egypt, out of the abode of slavery" (Ex. 20:2). God spoke these words, and ha-elohim (*the judges/God*, Ex. 21:6) are appointed to enact case law derived from the principles spoken at Sinai.

? Read Romans 12:19. *Explain how God oversees all activity and promises to intervene when the court fails.*
● *Suppose you are in the position of the downtrodden, and you encounter a judge who is not impartial. What do you do?*

Servanthood

❝ I am sending an angel ahead of you to guard you on the way and bring you to the place I have prepared. ❞

—*Exodus 23:20*

The first and second commandments spoken at Sinai are stressed in Sefer haB'rit's prologue and epilogue (Ex. 20:22-26(19-23 תנ״ך); 23:20-33, esp. 32-33) [Ramban, Ibn Ezra in Kaplan, p. 375; Durham, p. 334-337].

Covenant loyalty means momentous blessing.

The LORD's insistence upon absolute loyalty to Him comes as bookends to the Sefer haB'rit: No gods of silver and gold (Ex. 20:23(20 תנ״ך)) and no covenants with the Canaanites, lest they ensnare you to serve other gods (Ex. 23:32-33). Yisra'el is to be the LORD's eved (*servant, slave*) and the LORD's eved alone!

The LORD strictly admonishes Yisra'el: Sh'ma b'kolo (*Listen to His voice*, Ex. 23:21). Ki im shamo'a tish'ma b'kolo (*For if you indeed listen to* the angel of the LORD's *voice*), then God says, "I will be an enemy to your enemies" (Ex. 23:22). But this momentous blessing of angelic escort with no pity on enemies depends upon Yisra'el's servanthood to God, and to God alone.

? Read Ex. 9:1. ADONAI *implores: Shalach et-ami v'ya'avduni (Let My people go, so that they can serve/worship Me).* B'SHALACH *Par'oh (when Pharaoh let go), we were freed to serve in new ways. Discuss what serving God means.*

Prosperity

> **" In your land your women will not miscarry or be barren, and you will live out the full span of your lives. "**
>
> —*Exodus 23:26*

Momentous blessing means the promise of God's personal, providential care. The idyllic picture includes a burgeoning of blessings from Gan Eden.

All women will be fruitful (Gen. 1:28; Ex. 23:26), and Yisra'el will rule over her enemies! In fact, as God sent the wind to push back the deep (Ex. 14:21-22, 30-31), now God will send the hornet to scatter the enemies (Ex. 23:28).

But all these promises are based on chesed (*covenant loyalty*). There can be no idyllic blessings without chesed to God alone! Recall God's oath to Avraham: v'yirash zar'acha et-sha'ar o'y'vav ... ekev asher sh'ma'ta b'koli (*your seed will inherit the gates of his enemies ... as a result that you listened to My voice*, Gen. 22:17-18)!

> *Super-loyalty and super-obedience mean super-blessings from God.*

Now, the people ratify the covenant in blood (Ex. 24:3-8). First the altar is sprinkled. Then, words of Sefer haB'rit (*the Book of the Covenant*) are read aloud (Ex. 24:7), and the people are sprinkled as they respond, "Na'aseh v'nishma (*we will do and we will obey*)!"

? *Read Ex. 24:1, 3-8. As the people are cemented in blood, Moshe cries, "This is the blood of the covenant!" Give your reaction. Now read 1 Corinthians 11:25-26. Describe how the new covenant vicariously renews the first covenant.*

Entering God's Glory

> ❝ *Moshe entered the cloud and went up on the mountain; he was on the mountain forty days and nights.* ❞
>
> —*Exodus 24:18*

"**A**leh elai (*ascend to Me!*)," God commands (Ex. 24:12, 15). The cloud covers the mount, and Moshe prepares himself and then the people. After six days, on Shavuot with all the people watching, God calls Moshe to enter the cloud.

The holy are set apart to draw near to God.

Drawing near to God's glory and approaching Him in holiness are central to the summary. Yitro had covenanted with Elohim near the mountain and

returned home (Ex. 18:12). Now the leaders of Yisra'el covenant with God on the mount and are granted a vision on Mount Sinai (Ex. 24:9-11). Their covenant feast immediately follows the solemn covenant oath taken by all the people, who stand fenced off at the foot of the mountain (Ex. 24:3, 8).

But Moshe is called to Sinai's summit. He alone penetrates the mist from ha-shamayim (*the waters above*). He alone enters heaven's clouds. He alone fasts. Moshe remains in the mist upon the mount for forty days and forty nights.

? The sages say: *Ein mukdam oo-m'uchar baTorah* (there is no early or late in the Torah). The principle states that Torah does not always follow a chronological order. Do you think Moshe is on the mount in Ex. 25-31? Explain.

Reaffirming Covenant *Meander*

> **"** . . . *If I have not established my covenant with day and night and fixed the laws for sky and earth, then I will also reject the descendants of Ya'akov and of my servant David* . . . **"** — Jeremiah 33:25-26

Nebuchadnezzar invades Y'hudah and lays siege to the capital, Y'rushalayim. It is 589 BCE, and the end is near.

Yirm'yahu (*Jeremiah*) recalls the exodus from Egypt and quotes from the rishon of MISHPATIM, about setting free Hebrew slaves after seven years. In desperation, King Tsidkiyahu (*Zedekiah*) listens to Yirm'yahu, proclaims liberty to the slaves, and solemnizes the covenant (Jer. 34:8-10).

The siege is lifted and the people rejoice (588 BCE); but then the nobles decide that the Egyptian army had caused the pull back, and not the LORD. Nobles and people reverse course, taking back all their slaves (Jer. 34:11). It is the end.

> ## As long as day follows night, David's seed rules.

Tzidkiyahu's sons are killed in front of the king; and he is blinded, chained, and exiled into slavery. Says the LORD, he would reject the seed of David; but His covenant with day and night is based on His chukot (*statutes*), rules that go beyond reason (Jer. 33:25).

? Read Ex. 31:16-18. God fixed Shabbat as a time for rest with the seed of Yisra'el. Shabbat comes after day follows night for the sixth time. What is so special about resting on the seventh day? How is it related to David's seed?

> **"** *. . . Eliyahu is coming and will restore all things; on the other hand, I tell you that Eliyahu has come . . . the talmidim understood that he was talking . . . about Yochanan . . .* **"**   — *Matthew 17:11-13*

In the Days of Messiah, Yeshua stands on the Mt. of Transfiguration in the Land of Promise, with Peter, James, and John (Mt. 17:1).

It is six days since Yeshua has prophesied, ". . . some people standing here . . . will not experience death until they see the Son of Man coming in his Kingdom!" (Mt. 16:28; cf. Ex. 24:16-18, another 6-day wait). Suddenly, Messiah glows (Mt. 17:2-3)!

Once Moshe stood upon another mount, dying to enter the Land with his pleas apparently denied (Dt. 3:26-27a;

32:52; 34:5-6). Now, Moshe appears in the Land of Promise! Eliyahu, the herald who announces Messiah, also appears (Mt. 17:10-12; Mal. 4:5 (3:23 ך"נת)).

Moshe's hopes to enter the Land are fulfilled in the Days of Messiah.

As at Sinai, a bright cloud overshadows the witnesses and a voice calls out. It proclaims that Yeshua is God's Son: "Tishm'u elav (*Listen to Him*)!" (Mt. 17:5b; Dt. 18:15b). What validated Moshe as prophet now validates Yeshua.

? Read Mt. 17:13 (cf. Mt. 16:28). Yeshua's followers conclude that Yochanan comes to announce Messiah. Who would you say understood more about the Son of Man coming in His future Kingdom, Moshe or the followers?

Talk Your Walk . . .

Parashat MISHPATIM (*Judgments*) spells out Sefer haB'rit (*the Book of the Covenant*), instructing judges on case law for a society ruled by Torah. Rulings enact legislation derived from the founding principles, Aseret haDibrot (*the Ten Words/Utterances/ Commandments*) God spoke to all Yisra'el at Sinai.

Built upon the exodus from slavery, this society must always remember to protect the liberty of its citizens. Even those citizens who have hard-heartedly reduced themselves to slavery (by stealing, getting convicted in the courts, and then sold to pay their debts) are freed

> *The judge rules wisely, based on the Word of God.*

after the seventh year. Underlying principles such as freedom from oppression and compassion for the poor undergird the foundations of a society in covenant with the LORD.

Restitution or economic remedy must accompany apology for all offenses. Fair compensation, derived from case law, is derived from the principle of measure for measure. Where the rights of citizens conflict, the rights of the needy take precedence. However, judges are not to show partiality to protect the poor.

Rewards for covenant loyalty include momentous blessing. Super-loyalty and super-obedience are rewarded by super-blessings from God. An idyllic society can arise—Moshe in the clouds of heaven, and the hornets showing no pity to the enemies of Yisra'el!

Oasis

. . . Walk Your Talk

"**B**ut for now, three things last—trust, hope, love" (1 Cor. 13:13). Hope, God's vision of the future, guarantees eternity with God. Do you think it is possible to build your life on trust, hope, and love? Or do you live in the "real" world, where one must work for a living by the sweat of one's brow! Do you believe that man lives by bread alone? Yeshua quotes Torah, that one must also live "on every word that comes from the mouth of ADONAI" (Dt. 8:3; Mt. 4:4).

The children of Yisra'el did not work for a living in the wilderness. Their expenses zeroed out—clothes did not get holes, shoes did not wear out, and bread came to them straight from heaven. Do you desire such an idyllic existence?

Yet Yisra'el remained slow to trust and hope that God would, in fact, provide! Yisra'el found the idea of living the life of radical faith too scary. An idyllic life of sabbatical years (no work in year seven!) and jubilees (all debtors go free!) has never been voluntarily observed. Yet God promises that those who sow idealism based on His Word, will reap it—not only in the life to come, but in this "real" world too!

> *Walk in radical trust, step by step, and God will open up heaven on earth.*

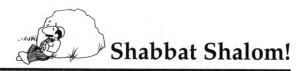 **Shabbat Shalom!**

God wants תרומה—
an offering, our gifts,
the kind bringing joy
to the one who uplifts—
for building a house
to dwell among you.
Then the whole world will know
He's God of the Jews!

"Make My throne in the Tabernacle
holy with gold.
Use the תרומה gifts,
make the cherubim bold.
Take the linen for the curtain,
twist it and fold
according to the plan
which I told you to hold."

Walk T'RUMAH!
25:1-27:19

Offering

TORAH—Exodus 25:1-27:19
- 1st Heartfelt Gifts—Exodus 25:1-2
- 2nd A Gold Cover—Exodus 25:17
- 3rd The M'norah—Exodus 25:31
- 4th Wood Planks—Exodus 26:15
- 5th Veiled Entrance—Exodus 26:31
- 6th A Copper Altar—Exodus 27:1
- 7th The Courtyard—Exodus 27:9
- Maftir Tabernacle Plans Complete!—Exodus 27:19

HAFTARAH—1 Kings 5:26-6:13
- Dwelling Within—1 Kings 6:13

B'RIT CHADASHAH—2 Corinthians 9:1-15
- Cheerful Givers—2 Corinthians 9:15

*Heartfelt Offerings
for the Tabernacle*

Hiker's

← Looking Back

B'REISHEET (*in the beginning*), God commands man to be fruitful, multiply, fill the earth, and subdue it. Man disobeys, choosing destruction, exile, and death.

> *These are our SH'MOT, Ya'akov's family, enslaved in Egypt. God tells Moshe, VA'ERA to keep My promises. Now BO! Negotiate with Pharaoh! B'SHALACH, our exodus begins. YITRO advises Moshe to appoint judges, who rule with wise MISHPATIM. And God requests T'RUMAH— our heartfelt offering!*

God covenants to redeem mankind through those who walk with Him. Chanoch is raptured alive; Noach and his household float on the deep, saved by grace while all life is judged. Avraham is promised offspring to bless all families of the world. God's covenant is passed across generations to Yisra'el, whose offspring will grow to nationhood.

The book of Exodus continues the story line: And these are the SH'MOT (*names*) of Ya'akov's sons, the royal family chosen by God. God blesses the family in exile, and their numbers grow. In desperation, Pharaoh resorts to slavery and then infanticide to contain the growth.

VA'ERA (*and I appeared*), says the LORD, to verify My promises to Avraham and redeem the nation from enslavement in Egypt. God tells Moshe, BO (*enter!*) and make final negotiations to free the sons of Yisra'el. Measure for measure, God punishes Pharaoh.

B'SHALACH Par'oh (*when Pharaoh let go*), God personally leads Yisra'el. Pharaoh, hardened one last time, gives chase to re-enslave the redeemed. God orders Moshe to split the

Log

sea! Egypt is hardened. The army follows Yisra'el, walking on the deep of the parted sea. The waters close, and the deep swallows the army! Yisra'el sees and believes. Then, on to Sinai!

YITRO (*Jethro*) advises Moshe to appoint a judiciary and to decide only the toughest cases. Yitro departs. Clouds gather over Sinai. On Shavuot, God speaks! People are agape! Then Moshe enters the cloud at the summit of Mount Sinai.

There, the LORD speaks words which Moshe records and reads aloud—the Sefer haB'rit (*Book of the Covenant*), instruction for making wise MISHPATIM (*judgments*). Based on the Ten Words spoken at Sinai, the principles protect personal freedom and require restitution for all wrongs.

In T'RUMAH . . .

The Key Person is Moshe (*Moses*), with the LORD.

The Scene is Har Sinai (*Mt. Sinai*).

Main Events include the LORD telling Moshe how to make the ark of the Testimony, the table of showbread, the lampstand, the tabernacle, the altar of burnt offering, the outer court, and the gate—all according to God's pattern and using precious materials offered by people with willing hearts.

Judges must be respected, even if they rule unfairly. The covenant is ratified, as the people and Sefer haB'rit are sprinkled with blood.

Moshe ascends for forty days and nights. Up on the mount, God instructs him to take T'RUMAH (an elevation *offering*) from the people to construct God's heavenly dwelling on the earth . . .

The Trail Ahead ➡

The Path

וידבר יהוה אל משה לאמר

דבר אל בני ישראל

ויקחו לי תרומה מאת כל איש

אשר ידבנו לבו

תקחו את תרומתי

—שמות כה/א-ב

ה	מָ	וּ	ר	תְּ
letter: hay	mem	vav	reish	tav
sound: H	**Mah**	OO	R	Tt'

offering = T'RUMAH = תרומה

Work

The Legend

and spoke the LORD	*va-y'daber ADONAI*	וַיְדַבֵּר יְהֹוָה
to Moses to say	*el-Mosheh lemor*	אֶל־מֹשֶׁה לֵּאמֹר׃
speak	*daber*	דַּבֵּר
to the sons of Israel	*el-b'nei Yisra'el*	אֶל־בְּנֵי יִשְׂרָאֵל
and they will take for me	*v'yik'chu-li*	וְיִקְחוּ־לִי
an <u>offering</u>	*t'rumah*	תְּרוּמָה
from every man	*me'et kol-eesh*	מֵאֵת כָּל־אִישׁ
that prompts him heart-his	*asher yid'venu libo*	אֲשֶׁר יִדְּבֶנּוּ לִבּוֹ
you will take	*tik'chu*	תִּקְחוּ
— <u>offering</u>-my	*et-t'rumati*	אֶת־תְּרוּמָתִי׃

—Exodus 25:1-2

Related Words

offering, donation, contribution, best part	*t'rumah*	תְּרוּמָה
oblation, offering, special offering	*t'rumiyah*	תְּרוּמִיָּה
lofty, noble, distinguished	*t'rumi*	תְּרוּמִי
to make a contribution, give the priestly tithe	*hevi (natan) t'rumah*	הֵבִיא (נָתַן) תְּרוּמָה
height, altitude	*room*	רוּם
high, lofty, eminent	*ram*	רָם
high place, height	*ramah*	רָמָה

Hit the Trail!

and Word Study
T'RUMAH • 123

Heartfelt Gifts

> ❝ ADONAI *said to Moshe, "Tell the people of Isra'el to take up a collection for me—accept a contribution from anyone who wholeheartedly wants to give."* ❞
> —*Exodus 25:1-2*

Says the LORD to Moshe on the mountaintop: take t'rumah (*an offering, elevated to a higher level*), a collective gift from people with generous and willing hearts. Build a mikdash (*sanctuary*) for Me from those gifts.

Accept gifts from those who deeply desire to give.

Only certain kinds of gifts are acceptable. These include gifts of gold, silver, and bronze; wools and linen; goat hair, ram skins, dolphin or sea cow skins; acacia wood; oils, spices, and incense; and onyx —all for making a sanctuary.

More importantly, only a certain kind of attitude on the part of the giver is acceptable. The reason goes beyond the fact that procuring what is needed is not difficult (Ex. 36:5-7). Rather, the people are no longer building something for Pharaoh, a severe task-master. The privilege of building something for God prolongs the joyous celebration of freedom. But the offerings must be given in such a way that the only intention is to glorify God. Nothing else!

? ● *Read Ex. 25:8, 1 Cor. 6:19-20. The Malbim (Meir Leib) observes that God dwells "among" the people, not "in" the mikdash (holy dwelling). Comment on his point that each person must build in his own heart a dwelling for God.*

A Gold Cover

❝ You are to make a cover for the ark out of pure gold; it is to be three-and-three-quarters feet long and two-and-a-quarter feet high. ❞

—Exodus 25:17

Straight to the throne room, the kapporet (*cover*) doubles for the footstool of God's throne and a seal for the top of the ark which will house the Ten Words on stone tablets.

> **The kapporet doubles for a cover and a footstool.**

The Holy of Holies is sometimes called the Room of the Kapporet (1 Chr. 28:11). There, the LORD speaks to Yisra'el from above the kapporet (Ex. 29:42-43; 30:6). In practice, the dwelling will be built before the ark [Ber. 55a; Ex. 36, 37]. However, the ark is described first, because it is more valued. The ark's cover is made from one ingot of solid gold, including the k'ruvim (*cherubim*) perched above.

Overshadowing the kapporet, the k'ruvim spread their wings, to protect and guard the way into the Most Holy Place (Ex. 25:20; Ez. 28:14-15). The k'ruvim face one another, gazing down at the kapporet with pure, childlike expressions, their wings protecting the LORD's face from sight.

Read Ps. 110:1, 4. God's throne is in mid-air, behind the outspread wings of the mysterious k'ruvim. There is no likeness nor representation where God sits. Who is David's Lord, and how can his enemies become his footstool?

The M'norah

> **"** *You are to make a menorah of pure gold. It is to be made of hammered work; its base, shaft, cups, ring of outer leaves and petals are to be of one piece with it.* **"**
>
> —*Exodus 25:31*

Instructions are given for making the golden m'norah to light the Holy Place. As with the golden cover for the ark, the m'norah is to be made from a single ingot of gold. Its branches, cups, knobs, and flowers are to be beaten out as a single, composite work.

> ### The m'norah is made as a single, unified work.

Making the m'norah perplexes Moshe [Tanch.]. Torah calls attention to Moshe's difficulty by using the word, tei'aseh (the m'norah, *she shall be made* beaten out, Ex. 25:31). The extra yod (תיעשה, not the usual passive, תעשה) has led some to say that B'tsal'el was told to throw the gold into the fire and out popped the m'norah [Mizrachi in Rashi, 1995, p. 336; cf. Ex. 32:24]!

Hareuveni [p. 137] observes that the m'norah closely resembles a wild sage plant—the salvia, also called the Judean moriah. The fragrant moriah plants exude a pleasing fragrance which has been likened to the speaking of the Ten Words [Shabb. 88b].

> **?** *Read Jn. 1:4, 9, 14. Each night, the m'norah is lit to shine in the Holy Place. The m'norah is a witness to Yisra'el and to the nations that the LORD spoke, calling Yisra'el to shine as a light. How does Yeshua embody this calling?*

Wood Planks

" Make the upright planks for the tabernacle out of acacia-wood. "

—Exodus 26:15

"Make the planks," takes a definite article, because planks with pedestals are used in the walls of divine dwellings in ancient near east cultures.

Make the planks for the walls of the inner tent.

The cosmic temple of the Canaanite god El had a mishkan (a word, in both Canaanite and Hebrew, meaning *dwelling*, a place for the Sh'chinah or *Presence* of God), with boards and pedestals [Cassuto, p. 323]. The mishkan included a throne with footstool, lamp, and table (the same holy furniture as in the LORD's tabernacle). However, in contrast to the LORD, who "neither slumbers nor sleeps" (Ps. 121:4), El's mishkan also housed a chest for clothes and a bed.

Each of the planks stands erect, with two tenons (hands) at the base to fix the boards into the silver pedestals. The planks were overlaid by gold and formed the perimeter of the mishkan, a rectangular area with interior dimensions 30 feet long and 15 feet wide.

? *Read Ex. 26:30. Do you think that the Canaanites saw Yisra'el's mishkan as El's celestial temple on earth?*
• *Explain how the sight of this dwelling would strike terror in the hearts of Canaanites.*

Veiled Entrance

❝ You are to make a curtain of blue, purple and scarlet yarn and finely woven linen. Make it with k'ruvim worked in, that have been crafted by a skilled artisan. ❞

—Exodus 26:31

Choshev (lit. *work of thought, skill; the finest, woven craftsmanship*) adorns the parochet (*partition, veil*), which divides the Holy from the Most Holy Place.

> ### The finest workmanship is reserved for the LORD.

The veil is suspended by gold hooks on top of four pillars that stand on silver pedestals. The principle of using the finest metals, the finest materials, and the finest of workmanship, when drawing near to the LORD is upheld in this striking approach to the entrance. The Holy Place could be entered only by a kohen in a state of ritual purity, either to perform a service of the mishkan or to prostrate in worship [Stone, p. 459].

The veil resembled the innermost overhead curtain, for both were made from the same materials, with the k'ruvim woven thoughtfully into both sides of the fabric. Inside the veil stood the Ark of the Covenant with kapporet and k'ruvim (*gold cover/footstool* and *cherubim*) all one piece in the throne room of the LORD!

? *Read Matthew 5:20. The principle that the finest workmanship and the best materials are reserved for proximity to the Most Holy Place applies to the standards for priests. Explain Yeshua's comment concerning righteousness.*

A Copper Altar

❝ You are to make the altar of acacia-wood, seven-and-a-half feet long and seven-and-a-half feet wide—the altar is to be square and four-and-a-half feet high. ❞

—Exodus 27:1

Atonement depends upon the blood service, thus the importance of the altar. Various names refer to the altar: the altar, the copper altar, the outer altar, and the altar of olah (*ascent offering*).

The outer altar is required for the blood service.

The altar effected a compromise between the altars of earth and stone (Ex. 20:24-25(21-22 תני״ך) and the fact that this altar was not meant to be temporary [Cassuto, p. 362].

Accordingly, the altar's planks and center were hollow, and could easily be filled with earth and stones, and upon which the kohanim would kindle the daily fire. The acacia wood was overlaid with bronze, lending permanence to this transportable altar.

Utensils for the altar included shovels and pots for removal of ashes, firepans for snatching coals to be conveyed to the inner altar or altar of incense, and forks with long handles and large prongs for arranging the flesh on the altar fire.

? *Read Ex. 27:2; 1 Ki. 1:50-53. According to the Talmud [Zev. 54a], horns were made on all four corners. Each horn measured a square cubit, and stood 5 handbreadths tall (18" x 18" x 15"). What was the purpose of the horns?*

The Courtyard

> **❝** *Here is how you are to make the courtyard of the tabernacle. On the south side, facing southward, are to be tapestries for the courtyard made of finely woven linen, 150 feet for one side.* **❞** —*Exodus 27:9*

Make a courtyard walled off by linen curtains suspended from rods attached to wooden pillars. These curtains are perforated, like a sieve, to allow wind to pass through [Rashi].

The woven work of the linens is not the choshev (*tight weaving*) adorning the veil or the covering. Rather, it is rokem (*a loose braiding*). These linens enclose a courtyard that measures 150' x 75' x 7.5'.

Entry to the courtyard is from the east. Set back at the center of the east side, a thirty foot screen allows entry on either side. Five pillars over-laid with gold support the outer screen, their hooks made of silver and their bases of copper. These materials contrast with the hooks of gold and bases of silver used on the four pillars which support the veil in front of the Most Holy Place.

The courtyard defines the limits of the sanctuary.

Only the ritually clean are permitted entry into the courtyard, because the courtyard determines the limits of the sanctuary precinct.

? *Read Dt. 22:11. The screen at the gate is made of the same mixture of wools and linens as the curtains overhead and the priestly garments as well. Called sha'atnez, Torah prohibits this mixture for private use. Explain.*

Tabernacle Plans Complete!

> ❝ *All the equipment needed for every kind of service in the tabernacle, as well as the tent pegs for the tabernacle and for the courtyard, are to be of bronze.* ❞
>
> —*Exodus 27:19*

Sixty pillars surround the 450 foot perimeter of the tabernacle area. Each pillar stands on a copper base, its top filleted with silver. The pillars are 7.5 feet high.

The outer altar stands in the center of the eastern half of the court. Cassuto [p. 365] speculates that the ark's position is central to the western half of the court.

The western half of the court measures 75' x 75'. The inner tent, consisting of the Holy Place and Most Holy Place measures 45' x 45', leaving a 30' distance between the inner tent and the walls of the courtyard. Within the area, bronze pegs pounded into the ground secure the overhead curtains of ram skins and tachashim (*dolphin/sea cow*).

The plan describing the tabernacle is completed.

The pounding of the pegs finishes the work of the mikdash (*tabernacle*). The shvi'i segment reviews twelve of the thirteen gifts that qualify as t'rumah (an elevation *offering*). The only item not mentioned is gold!

❓ *Read Is. 33:20, 22. The future Y'rushalayim is liberated from the yoke of a foreign super-power. Now, ADONAI rules as judge and king. Tsiyon is a tent that cannot be pulled up, whose pegs can never be uprooted. Explain.*

Dwelling Within   *Meander*

> ❝ *I will live in it among the people of Isra'el, and I will not abandon my people Isra'el.* ❞
>
> — *1 Kings 6:13*

Building a sanctuary dominates both the parashah and its Haftarah. In both instances, the purpose is the same: that God may dwell among His people.

Most glaring is the contrast between the LORD's way of receiving t'rumah (an elevation *offering*) from willing hearts and Solomon's way of conscripting forced labor (1 Ki. 5:13 (27 תְּמַ"רְ)). Hertz [p. 336] observes that King Solomon's ways finally tear the kingdom apart!

The LORD's words to Shlomo still ring true today: ". . . if you will live according to my regulations, follow my rulings and observe all my mitzvot and live by them, then I will establish with you my promise . . . I will live . . . among the people of Isra'el, and I will not abandon my people Isra'el" (1 Ki. 6:12-13).

The LORD *dwells among those who observe Torah.*

What sustains God's Presence is the willingness to submit one's life and conduct to guidance under Torah—not the sanctuary built as a reminder of His Presence among us!

? *The mishkan was erected in 2449. The temple was started in 2928, finished in 2935, and destroyed in 3338. The mishkan was temporary, but the temple was supposed to be permanent. Why did God dwell longer in the mishkan?*

> ❝ *Thanks be to God for his indescribable gift!* ❞
> — *2 Corinthians 9:15*

Cheerful giving "overflows into the thanks that people give to God" (2 Cor. 9:12). Not only are the needs of God's people being met, but the gift multiplies the praises God receives when the recipients of such gifts return glory to God!

> **Cheerful givers multiply the glory God receives.**

Rav Sha'ul urges the Corinthians to give to the poor in Jerusalem, but not grudgingly or with compulsion (2 Cor. 9:7a). He reminds the Corinthians that their mere pledge to the Jerusalem Fund stirred up the poor of Macedonia to give generously and beyond their means (2 Cor. 8:3-4). Indeed, the Macedonians gave more than money—they gave of themselves (2 Cor. 8:5).

Rav Sha'ul insists that the importance of generous giving is two-fold: God will supply the means (2 Cor. 9:6-10; cf. Dt. 8:7-10), and the results of generosity redound to the Glory of God (2 Cor. 9:11-15). The humble person who exalts the LORD will be lifted up.

? *The Septuagint translates Proverbs 22:9a as, "God blesses a cheerful and giving man" (cf. 2 Cor. 9:7b). Explain how cheerful giving can stimulate others to glorify God. Relate cheerful giving to the concept of T'rumah.*

Talk Your Walk . . .

The LORD tells Moshe how to build the ark of the Testimony, the footstool including the k'ruvim (*cherubim*), the m'norah, the table of showbread, the inner tabernacle, the copper altar, the veil of partition, the outer court, and the gate—all according to God's pattern, using specified precious materials to be offered by people with willing hearts. The LORD tells Moshe to take T'RUMAH (an elevation *offering*) from those with willing hearts. Giving the gifts solely for the glory of the LORD elevates the donors and the nation!

> *Receive heartfelt gifts to build My dwelling place.*

God gives a plan for constructing the mikdash (*tabernacle*). He promises to meet with the people from within the mishkan (*tent of His glorious Presence*). Inside the Most Holy Place stands the ark with a gold covering. This lid doubles for the footstool in God's throne room and the seal for the Ten Words spoken at Sinai and later written on stone tablets to be sealed inside the Ark.

God promises to dwell among His people. He promises His glorious Presence, so long as His people are faithful to His covenant, keep His statutes and mishpatim (*judgments*), and commit to a life of holiness. The mishkan, then, is not a tent for carrying God. Rather, it is a conscious reminder to the people that a holy God spoke to them at Sinai and that He is still present among them this very day.

Oasis

. . . Walk Your Talk

T'RUMAH (an elevation *offering*) is collected from the people in order to build the mikdash—the central rallying point for the Presence of the LORD among His people. Once built, the tabernacle will be encircled by holy and ritually clean kohanim, ringed by the tribes, and topped by the cloud of God's Presence. The moving tabernacle is a picture of Sinai.

God accepted t'rumah only from those who gave purely for the sake of glorifying Him in their midst! It is a spiritual fact of life that those who give with the sole and unselfish intention of glorifying God are themselves elevated at that very moment. At Sinai, elders and kohanim

> *God elevates those who seek to glorify Him.*

were called up the mountain. Moshe was elevated to the summit, as he entered the cloud and did not eat for forty days and nights!

The one who seeks to give glory to the LORD draws near to God with a power that transforms life! Do you seek to glorify God? Look to your motives, and remove the taint of personal concerns. Picture the cherubim. When your eyes focus steadfastly upon the mercy seat to multiply His glory, your feet will rise from the ground—but you won't have time to notice!

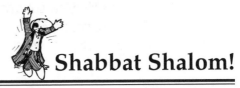 **Shabbat Shalom!**

Now God said to Moshe,
"תצוה!"
Command Yisra'el
to light the way.
Install the priests
to keep it shining each day.
Light the wicks at evening!
Remember to pray!

Near the altar of incense
I promise to abide.
Yes, in the smoke
My glory will hide!
Make holy the priests,
so they're sanctified
to approach Me in prayer
and burn incense inside.

Walk T'TSAVEH!
27:20-30:10

You shall command

TORAH—Exodus 27:20-30:10
- 1st Command Purity—Exodus 27:20
- 2nd Mount the Stones—Exodus 28:13-14
- 3rd Priestly Robes—Exodus 28:31
- 4th Preparing Kohanim—Exodus 29:1
- 5th Consecrating the Kohanim—Exodus 29:19-20
- 6th Daily Offerings—Exodus 29:38
- 7th Daily Incense—Exodus 30:1
- Maftir Yearly Atonement—Exodus 30:10

HAFTARAH—Ezekiel 43:10-27
- Reconsecrated Eighth—Ezekiel 43:27

B'RIT CHADASHAH—Hebrews 13:10-16
- Continue Daily Offerings—Hebrews 13:16

Command Yisra'el
to Light God's Dwelling

← Looking Back

B'REISHEET (*in the beginning*), God creates Gan Eden (*the Garden of Eden, paradise*) and puts Adam there to be present with Him in His unfinished creation. God initiates the work of redemption after the death of Hevel (*Abel*) by *appointing* Shet (*Seth*) as replacement. The tenth generation of Shet is Noach's son, Shem (*name*), the start of passing a heritage of monotheism through the Shemite priesthood. The sons of Avraham, Yitzchak, and Ya'akov (renamed Yisra'el) will be called to this priesthood.

Exodus begins: these are the SH'MOT (*names*) of Ya'akov's sons, whom God blesses to be fruitful. They multiply exceedingly, fill the land of Goshen, and threaten the empire of Egypt.

Pharaoh oppresses them to stop their growth.

VA'ERA (*and I appeared*), says the LORD, to make good on promises to Avraham to liberate the sons of Yisra'el and lead them back to possess the Land of C'na'an (*Canaan*).

These are the SH'MOT of sons enslaved in Egypt. VA'ERA as promised, says God. Now BO, negotiate with Pharaoh! B'SHALACH, God leads us out. YITRO advises Moshe to appoint judges, who hear God's wise MISHPATIM read aloud. On the mount, God tells Moshe: Collect T'RUMAH for My Dwelling, and T'TSAVEH—you shall command My people to keep the light!

God tells Moshe, BO (*enter!*) and negotiate to free the sons of Yisra'el. God pun-

Log

ishes Pharaoh, measure for measure. **B'SHALACH** Par'oh (*when Pharaoh let go*), God leads Yisra'el with His Presence. Near Sinai, father-in-law **YITRO** (*Jethro*) advises Moshe to delegate legal cases to a judiciary. The Sefer haB'rit (*Book of the Covenant*) is read to all. It instructs judges on making wise **MISHPATIM** (*judgments*). Atop Mt. Sinai, Moshe is told to take **T'RUMAH** (*an offering*) to elevate the nation and build a dwelling for God's Presence.

Instruction continues: **T'TSAVEH** (*you shall command*) Yisra'el to keep a light burning in the darkness. The nation is consecrated for holy service. Holiness includes proper attire, so special vestments are prepared for the priests. The Kohen Gadol (*High Priest*) sacrifices a bull before entering, for it is not

---

In T'TSAVEH . . .
The Key Person is Moshe (*Moses*), with the LORD.
The Scene is Har Sinai (*Mt. Sinai*).
Main Events include God continuing to instruct Moshe about tabernacle service, including the eternal light, dressing the priests (Aharon and sons), consecrating them, how they shall offer sacrifices, and how to make the altar of incense.

---

possible to enter God's Holy Presence without the shedding of blood.

Further commands spell out a special ceremony for consecrating priests. Thereafter, daily offerings will start and end each day. Each year on Yom Kippur, the High Priest cleanses the altars to preserve holiness. Should the sins of the nation pile up on the altar without atonement, the Presence of God could be driven out of the camp . . .

The Trail Ahead

Compass

The Path

ואתה תצוה את בני ישראל
ויקחו אליך שמן זית זך
כתית למאור
להעלת נר תמיד

—שמות כז/כ

letter:	hay	vav	tsadee	tav
	ה	וִ	צַ	תְ
sound:	H	**Vveh**	TSah	Tt'

you shall command = **T'TSAVEH** = תצוה

Work

The Legend

and you	*v'atah*	וְאַתָּה
you shall command	*t'tsaveh*	תְּצַוֶּה
— sons of Israel	*et-b'nei Yisra'el*	אֶת־בְּנֵי יִשְׂרָאֵל
& they will take to you	*v'yik'chu eleicha*	וְיִקְחוּ אֵלֶיךָ
oil (of) olive	*shemen zayit*	שֶׁמֶן זַיִת
pure, pressed	*zach katit*	זָךְ כָּתִית
for the light	*la-ma'or*	לַמָּאוֹר
to go up	*l'ha'alot*	לְהַעֲלֹת
light eternal	*ner tamid*	נֵר תָּמִיד:

—*Exodus 27:20*

Related Words

command, order, law, precept	*tsav*	צַו
will, testament, order	*tsava'ah*	צַוָּאָה
need (command) of the hour	*tsav ha-sha'ah*	צַו הַשָּׁעָה
commandment(s)	*mitsvah, mitsvot*	מִצְוָה, מִצְוֹת
son of the commandment	*bar-mitsvah*	בַּר־מִצְוָה
daughter of the commandment	*bat-mitsvah*	בַּת־מִצְוָה
who sanctified us	*asher kid'shanu*	אֲשֶׁר קִדְּשָׁנוּ
by His commands	*b'mitsvotav*	בְּמִצְוֹתָיו
and commanded us to kindle	*v'tsivanu l'hadlik*	וְצִוָּנוּ לְהַדְלִיק
(the) candle(s) of Sabbath	*ner shel shabbat*	נֵר שֶׁל שַׁבָּת

Hit the Trail!

Command Purity

❝ *You are to order the people of Isra'el to bring you pure oil of pounded olives for the light, and to keep a lamp burning continually.* ❞

—*Exodus 27:20*

Moshe receives direct orders to collect clear oil for making the purest light. The finest drippings—shemen zayit zach katit (*oil of olive, pure, pressed*) —are gathered from the first droplets oozing from plump, ripe olives (Ex. 27:20).

The LORD *commands light to shine through the night.*

The olive oil is hand crushed in a mortar [Rashi, Men. 86b], not ground by mill stone. This careful, labor intensive procedure prevents olive particles from muddying the clarity of virgin olive oil. The unwavering, smokeless, translucent light shines brilliantly from the m'norah in the Holy Place. Shining through the night, the ner tamid (*eternal light*) pictures Yisra'el as a nation to bring light to the nations [Hertz, p. 339; Is. 42:6].

God commands Aharon and his sons to light the ner tamid each evening, as an everlasting statute (Ex. 27:21). The next morning, Aharon renews the wicks, refills the lamp with oil, and prepares for evening.

? *Read Matthew 5:14-16. In what way have the priestly duties to be a light to the nations been assumed by believers? Give some examples of where the fruits of your faith have led to good deeds that witness to others.*

Mount the Stones

> " Make gold squares and two chains of pure gold,
> twisted like cords; attach the cord-like chains to the
> squares. "
>
> —Exodus 28:13-14

Onyx stones are mounted in the gold squares that Aharon bears upon his shoulders. As he walks into the Presence of the LORD, the names of the sons of Yisra'el—engraved upon the stones—can be read vertically by the LORD as a zikaron (*reminder*, Ex. 28:12).

Engraved stones are reminders that Yisra'el is set apart for the LORD.

Gold cords are attached to the square settings and then to shoulder straps which secure the breastplate. Mounted upon the breastplate are twelve precious stones, each engraved with the name of one of the tribes of Yisra'el. The Kohen Gadol (*High Priest*) enters the LORD's Presence bearing the names of the tribes upon his heart.

Underneath the breastplate, or possibly within its fold, are the Urim and Tumim (*lightings* and *perfections*), devices for receiving prophetic direction. As the High Priest meditates upon questions asked of the LORD, Talmud says the High Priest is elevated to divine inspiration [Yo. 73b].

Read Gen. 46:8-27; Ex. 1:1-5. Notice the names of the twelve sons of Yisra'el on the onyx stones and on the breastplate. Why are the names of Levi and Yosef engraved upon the stones, rather than Efrayim and M'nasheh?

Priestly Robes

Vesting the Kohen Gadol (*High Priest*) in proper attire is critical for approaching the LORD.

**Proper vestment
is required
to approach the LORD.**

Four vestments resemble those of ordinary priests (coat, girdle, turban, and tunic). Four additional garments distinguish the Kohen Gadol: the ephod (*apron*), choshen (*breastplate*), tsits (*gold headplate*), and m'il (*robe made of blue wool*).

The m'il is finely woven in one piece, symbolizing integrity. Its blue color comes from the same rare dye used to make the blue thread of t'fillin.

The robe is slipped overhead and hugs the body down to the feet. It is worn under the ephod and the choshen. Near the feet, the hem is embroidered with pomegranates and golden bells—36 or 72 pomegranates in all [Zev. 88b, Ex. 28:33]. The bells tinkle so people will know when the Kohen Gadol enters the Holy of Holies to intercede before the LORD.

? Read Ephesians 4:24. Explain how New Covenant believers can clothe themselves *"with the new nature ... which expresses itself in the righteousness and holiness that flow from truth."* How can you dress in this spiritual attire?

Preparing Kohanim

❝ Here is what you are to do to consecrate them for ministry to me in the office of cohen. Take one young bull and two rams without defect . . . ❞

—Exodus 29:1

Milu'im (*consecration*) of the priests will actually occur from 23 Adar to 1 Nisan [Stone, p. 474]. Here, the commands Moshe receives focus on clothing, anointing, laying hands upon, and sanctifying Aharon.

The LORD commands Moshe to consecrate Aharon and his sons.

The ceremony elevates Aharon and his sons to perform the service of the sanctuary. Ordination mandates priests, literally "fills their hands," for service.

The ceremony of dedication begins with the command to sacrifice a young bull and two rams at the door of the ohel moed (*tent of meeting*). Aharon and sons present a basket of bread, flat cakes, and wafers of matzah. Then they wash at mikveh [Rashi]. Investiture follows (cf. Lev. 8:7-9, 13). The priests are clothed, anointed, and ordained (mandated, Ex. 29:9). They confess personal sins, and the bull is slaughtered. The blood is used to anoint the horns of the altar. The flesh, hide, and offal are burned outside the camp.

Read Hebrews 13:11-13. Is the author of Hebrews describing the death of Yeshua as a sin offering? Explain the implications for consecrating a priesthood of New Covenant believers from all nations of the world.

Consecrating the Kohanim

❝ *Take the other ram: Aharon and his sons are to lay their hands on the ram's head; and you are to slaughter the ram, take some of its blood, and put it on the lobe of Aharon's right ear . . .* **❞**   —*Exodus 29:19-20*

Commands for preparatory rites of induction given at this time are carried out in Lev. 8-10. First, a ram must be slaughtered as an olah (*ascent offering*), its blood dashed on the four corners of the altar, and the rest burned.

A second ram, the ram of ordination, is to be slain immediately after Aharon and his sons place their hands on its head and perform vidui (*confession*). Its blood must be applied to Aharon's right ear lobe, right thumb, and right big toe. The symbolic meaning is self-evi-dent—that the kohen have ears to hear God's word, hands to perform priestly duties, and feet to walk in righteousness (Ex. 29:20).

> **The ram of ordination will elevate the kohanim for service.**

The ram of ordination will be waved before the Lord, its breast and thigh eaten with bread as zivchei sh'lamim (*completion offerings*) at a closed communion meal. The leftovers must then be burned (Ex. 29:32-34).

? *Read John 6:48-59, especially Jn. 6:51-54. Perhaps Yeshua is offering to consecrate his students. What made this such a "hard word" among his talmidim? Explain why so many left Him, and only the twelve remained (Jn. 6:66).*

Daily Offerings

" Now this is what you are to offer on the altar: two lambs a year old, regularly, every day. "

—Exodus 29:38

For seven days, bulls are offered as a chata't (*sin offering*) to sanctify the altar (Ex. 29:37). The outer altar is now called Kodesh Kodashim (*Holy of Holies*).

The nation starts and ends the day with gifts to God who dwells among them.

The chief duty of the newly consecrated kohanim is to start the day and end the night with the olat tamid (*daily/regular ascent offering*). According to Kennedy, the "tamid" is "the center and core of public worship" in Judaism [Hertz, Num. 28:6]. At the altar, God promises to meet with Yisra'el (Ex. 29:43).

No gifts could be offered to God before the morning tamid or after the late afternoon tamid. In this way, the nation always started and ended the day with gifts. Accompanying the daily offerings were two quarts of fine flour mixed with olive oil and a quart of wine. In return, the LORD promises to speak—the proof of Presence once demanded by Pharaoh has become a Promise of Presence at God's dwelling (Ex. 29:45-46).

? Review Ex. 24:5. At Sinai, those who made offerings to the LORD started with the olah. Do you think there is a remembrance of Sinai built into the olat tamid? How does God's response (Ex. 29:43-46) also fit into this picture?

Daily Incense

❝ *You are to make an altar on which to burn incense; make it of acacia-wood.* ❞

—*Exodus 30:1*

Altar construction seems to belong in the previous portion, describing furnishings for the sanctuary. The mention of the golden altar, placed here at the conclusion of commands regarding priestly vestments and ritual, is deliberate.

Each day, Yisra'el renews the glorious praise of meeting God at Sinai.

The incense altar has no equivalent in the celestial abodes of Canaanite deities. Nor are sacrifices allowed on this altar (Ex. 30:9).

Yet evening to evening, b'ha'alot Aharon (*Aaron causes to go up*) the light of the lamps at the same time yaktirenah (*he causes to send up in smoke*) incense upon the altar of gold (Ex. 30:7-8).

Again the picture of Sinai is splendidly portrayed. The people stand before the sanctuary, which is fenced off. Inside the courts stands the ohel moed (*tent of meeting*), where Aharon and his sons ascend. Closer still and higher yet rises the Kohen Gadol—to cause light to ascend in a cloud of smoke to meet with the LORD.

? *Recall that gold is not mentioned in the maftir which summarizes T'RUMAH (offerings) for the sanctuary (Ex. 27:17-19). Picture the Most Holy, from the vantage point of God, and describe the golden forms visible to you.*

Yearly Atonement

" Aharon is to make atonement on its horns once a year—with the blood of the sin offering of atonement . . . once a year through all your generations; it is especially holy to ADONAI. "   —Exodus 30:10

The goal and purpose of sacrifices is two-fold: (1) God dwells among Yisra'el and demands a holy camp (Ex. 25:8-9); and (2) God descends in His glory to meet with Yisra'el at the ohel moed (*tent of meeting*), which He alone sanctifies (Ex. 29:43-46).

> **The holiness of the golden altar is preserved yearly.**

To keep the camp clean, yearly atonement is made on the golden altar (Ex. 30:10). The atonement must be made by application of the blood of the chata't (*sin offering*) upon the horns of the golden altar on Yom Kippur [Lev. 16:18; Rashi; Yoma 61a]. One might wonder why it is so important to cleanse an altar upon which no sacrifices are allowed (Ex. 30:9). Describing the purpose of the incense offering, Sforno [p.443] quotes Tanchuma: "The incense offering does not come to expiate sin or transgression of guilt. It comes only to bring simchah (joy or happiness)." Thus, the purpose of incense is to honor God after He comes and to welcome His Presence (cf. 1 Chr. 16:29).

? *Read Psalm 141:2, which describes prayer as incense. The rabbis characterize K'TORET (incense) in terms of prayer:*
• *K'dushah (holiness), T'horah (purity), Rachamim (compassion), and Tikvah (hope). What characterizes your prayer?*

Reconsecrated Eighth *Meander*

> ❝ *"When these days are over, then, on the eighth day and afterwards, the cohanim will present your burnt offerings on the altar and your peace offerings; and I will accept you," says Adonai* ELOHIM. ❞ —Ez. 43:27

Coming in the midst of Ezekiel's vision of New Jerusalem, this particular chapter (Ez. 43) describes God's return to the temple. But it is not the second temple, it is the temple to come [Radak]!

The prophet sees Yisra'el re-enacting the Sinai covenant in the Land.

Parallel with the consecration of the copper altar in the parashah (Ex. 29:36-37), Yechezk'el (*Ezekiel*) requires that a chata't (*sin offering*) be offered each day, for seven days, to cleanse the altar. Then the altar is anointed, sanctified as most holy (Ez. 43:26-27).

Yisra'el will not pollute this temple as they polluted the former temple (Ez. 44:6-10). Indeed, only Zadokites will serve (these are priests who remained loyal to David, Ez. 44:15-16).

In this vision, Yechezk'el is mystically transported from exile to Y'rushalayim (Ez. 40:1-4). One can wonder which kohanim will be transported and consecrated to "present your burnt offerings on the altar and your peace offerings" (Ez. 43:27).

? *Read Ex. 24:3-11. Notice that our people ratified Sefer haB'rit (Book of the Covenant) in blood, and that young men made offerings in the Presence of God. Explain how redeeming the nation requires a cleansed altar in the Land.*

...*ings*   Continue Daily Offerings

> **" But don't forget doing good and sharing with others, for with such sacrifices God is well pleased. "**
>
> — *Hebrews 13:16*

Motives "for doing good and sharing with others" (Heb. 13:16) should not be entangled with desires for the respect or acceptance of others, but solely to please God. Believers "must not seek respect or inclusion on any terms except God's" [Stern, 1992, p. 722].

Yeshua's sacrifice, taking place "outside the camp," is perceived by the world as "disgraceful"(Heb. 13:11-13). If Yeshua couldn't avoid such disgrace when sacrificing to please God, how should we expect anything different?

The rabbis point to fulfillment of the covenant sacrifices: "In the time to come, all sacrifices will be annulled except for the sacrifice of thanksgiving" [Lev. R. 9:7].

Gifts of praise and thanksgiving characterize life in the time to come.

These special sacrifices are called todah (*thank offerings*) (Jer. 33:11), special sh'lamim (*fellowship* or *peace offerings*) eaten in one day (cf. Jn. 6:50-59). Though mysterious, we share His disgrace in order to appropriate His grace.

Read Ps. 51:17-18, 21 (15-16, 19 תגד), Ro. 12:1-2, Heb. 13:16. Distinguish the offerings that are acceptable on the golden altar from the offerings that the nations might bring. What sacrifices will be acceptable at the temple?

Talk Your Walk . . .

I n the clouds for forty days and forty nights, Moshe receives divine instruction concerning the dwelling that Yisra'el will build from the t'rumot (elevation *offerings*). God commands him: atah t't-saveh (*you shall command*) the Israelites to keep the ohel moed (*tent of meeting*) lit all night, every night.

This important task shall be entrusted to Aharon and his sons. To prepare them for this ministry, they are set apart as represen-tatives of the nation and given special priestly clothing. These priests will be consecrated for a seven-day period and installed in the office of kohan-im ba-yom ha-SH'MINI (*on the eighth day*). Both the priests and the altar must be consecrated and elevated for ministry. Instructions given to Moshe at this time will be carried out in the book of Leviticus.

> **Kohanim are elevated to re-enact the mystery of drawing near to the LORD.**

The Kohen Gadol (*High Priest*) is specially equipped, with Urim and Tumim, to ascend closer still and to receive divine responses to questions affecting the welfare of the community as a whole. Yisra'el responds through its priestly representatives by offering sweet k'toret (*incense*) of praise and fer-vent prayer characterized by k'dushah (*holiness*), t'horah (*purity*), rachamim (*compassion*), and tikvah (*hope*). These prayers ascend with the incense over the screen and into the Most Holy Place of the One Who dwells in the midst of His people.

Oasis

. . . Walk Your Talk

Collecting t'rumot (elevation *offerings*) for God's dwelling raises up Yisra'el as a priestly nation that serves the LORD. These offerings are then designated as sh'lamim (*fellowship* or *peace offerings*), which are given to Aharon and his sons for all time (Ex. 29:28). When the priest eats the t'rumah from the chata't and asham (*sin* and *guilt offerings*) within the mikdash (*holy dwelling*), he relives the sacrificial meal of Aharon and his sons at their installation (Ex. 29:31-34). This installation itself is a living re-enactment of the feast between God and the elders of Yisra'el at Mount Sinai during the inauguration of the covenant.

The priest's eating of the ram and the bread completes the atonement of the worshipper, who comes to the altar seeking forgiveness of sins. Yeshua referred to this understanding of Torah. He speaks directly to his followers, saying that they can have no lasting relation with Him

New Covenant priests are elevated to a life of service and walking with Yeshua.

unless they eat flesh and bread that comes from heaven (Jn. 6:50-51). Over this statement, all of Yeshua's students leave, except for the twelve. Even today, eating Messiah's supper elevates New Covenant priests for holy service and walking with Him (Jn. 6:66).

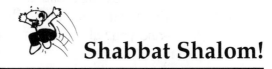

Shabbat Shalom!

כי תשא,
"when you elevate,"
pay one-half shekel
to redeem, not forsake.
Use the silver for parts—
God's house you'll make.
Draw near to the LORD,
for goodness sake!

Do not make images—
avoid them for sure.
No golden calf,
just keep yourselves pure!
No treaties with Canaan,
'cuz idols allure.
Keep your eyes on haShem,
and your glow will endure!

Walk Kɪ Tɪsᴀ!
30:11-34:35

When you elevate

Toʀᴀʜ—Exodus 30:11-34:35
   1st Elevate All Donors—Exodus 30:11-12
   2nd God-Given Tablets—Exodus 31:18
   3rd Be Present Among Us—Exodus 33:12
   4th Behold, the Presence!—Exodus 33:17-18
   5th Man-Made Tablets—Exodus 34:1
   6th The Nation Elevated—Exodus 34:10
   7th Covenant Renewed—Exodus 34:27
   Maftir Glowing for God—Exodus 34:35

Hᴀꜰᴛᴀʀᴀʜ—1 Kings 18:1-39
   Presence Manifested—1 Kings 18:39

Bʀɪᴛ Cʜᴀᴅᴀsʜᴀʜ—2 Corinthians 3:1-18
   Radiating in God's Glory—2 Corinthians 3:18

When You Elevate . . .
Your Light Shines for God

◀ Looking Back

B'REISHEET (*in the beginning*) God created Gan Eden (*Garden of Eden, paradise*) and put Adam there to be present with Him in His unfinished creation. Adam chooses to disobey, and his firstborn, Kayin, succumbs to sibling rivalry and murders his brother. God curses Kayin for murder, and later, God curses C'na'an. Torah does not give reasons, but tradition says that C'na'an stood by his father when Ham disrespectfully looked upon his father's nakedness. Later, God will raise up a nation to redeem C'na'an from fertility cults and abominations.

Exodus begins: and these are the SH'MOT (*names*) of Ya'akov's sons, whom God blesses to be fruitful. They multiply exceedingly, fill the land of Goshen, and threaten the empire of Egypt. To stop their growth, Pharaoh oppresses them.

VA'ERA (*and I appeared*), says the LORD, to make good on promises to Avraham, to free the sons of Yisra'el and lead them back to possess C'na'an.

These are the SH'MOT
of Ya'akov's growing family,
enslaved in Egypt.
God tells Moshe, VA'ERA . . .
BO! Free My people
from Pharaoh! B'SHALACH,
the sea parts before us.
YITRO rejoices, then advises:
Appoint judges to govern
by God's wise MISHPATIM.
God says: Take heartfelt T'RUMAH
for building My dwelling, and
T'TSAVEH My people
to keep the light.
KI TISA—when you elevate to
holy service, follow God to the top!

God tells Moshe, **BO** (*enter!*) and negotiate to free the sons of Yisra'el. God punishes Pharaoh, measure for

Log

measure. **B'SHALACH** Par'oh (*when Pharaoh let go*), God leads Yisra'el with His Presence.

Near Sinai, Moshe's father-in-law **YITRO** (*Jethro*) advises Moshe to delegate legal cases to a judiciary. The Sefer haB'rit (*Book of the Covenant*) instructs judges to make wise **MISHPATIM** (*judgments*). God tells Moshe to take **T'RUMAH** (*offering*) and elevate the nation to build a dwelling for His Presence. He adds, **T'TSAVEH** (*you shall command*) Yisra'el to tend the light in the night. God instructs the priestly nation on how they will approach Him in His holiness.

Now God orders a census: **KI TISA** (*when you elevate*) the nation to holy service in the army, let each man pay a silver coin to atone

In KI TISA . . .

The Key People are Moshe (*Moses*), B'tsal'el (*Bezalel*), Oholi'av (*Oholiab*), people of Yisra'el (*Israel*), Aharon (*Aaron*), and Y'hoshua (*Joshua*).

The Scenes include Har Sinai (*Mt. Sinai*) and the camp nearby.

Main Events include instructions for census and atonement money; artisans filled with God's Spirit; reminder to keep Shabbat; stone tablets, golden calf, Lord's anger, Moshe pleading, tablets broken, people punished, Aharon's excuses, Levites to Lord's side, 3000 killed in camp; return to mountain, seeking forgiveness; plague; Moshe's tent, meeting God's glory, cutting new tablets; God's covenant to do marvels, warning against alliances, commanding pilgrimages, Moshe's face shining, and putting on veil.

for his life in advance of the holy war to redeem the Land of C'na'an . . .

The Trail Ahead

Compass

The Path

וַיְדַבֵּר יהוה אֶל מֹשֶׁה לֵּאמֹר

כִּי תִשָּׂא אֶת רֹאשׁ בְּנֵי יִשְׂרָאֵל

לִפְקֻדֵיהֶם

וְנָתְנוּ אִישׁ כֹּפֶר נַפְשׁוֹ לַיהוה

בִּפְקֹד אֹתָם

וְלֹא יִהְיֶה בָהֶם נֶגֶף

בִּפְקֹד אֹתָם

—שמות ל/יא

letter:	א alef	שָׁ sin	תָ tav		י yod	כִּ kaf
sound:	(silent)	**Ssah**	Tee		EE	Kee

when you elevate = **KI TISA** = **כִּי תִשָּׂא**

Work

The Legend

and spoke the LORD	va-y'daber ADONAI	וַיְדַבֵּר יְהוָה
to Moses to say	el Mosheh lemor	אֶל־מֹשֶׁה לֵּאמֹר:
when you elevate	ki tisa	כִּי תִשָּׂא
— head(s) of sons of Israel	et-rosh b'nei-Yisra'el	אֶת־רֹאשׁ בְּנֵי־יִשְׂרָאֵל
to count them	lif'kudeihem	לִפְקֻדֵיהֶם
then will give man	v'nat'noo eesh	וְנָתְנוּ אִישׁ
a covering for soul-his	kofer nafsho	כֹּפֶר נַפְשׁוֹ
to the LORD in counting them	la-ADONAI bifkod otam	לַיהוָה בִּפְקֹד אֹתָם
so not will be among them	v'lo-yih'yeh va-hem	וְלֹא־יִהְיֶה בָהֶם
a plague when counting them	negef bifkod otam	נֶגֶף בִּפְקֹד אֹתָם:

—Exodus 30:11

Related Words

to take a wife	nasa isha	נָשָׂא אִשָּׁה
married	nasui	נָשׂוּי
to take an oath (raise his hand)	nasa yado	נָשָׂא יָדוֹ
to volunteer (elevated his heart)	n'sao libo	נָשְׂאוּ לִבּוֹ
to carry/bear/use arms	nasa neshek	נָשָׂא נֶשֶׁק
leader, chief, ruler, captain (elevated one)	nasee	נָשִׂיא
to count, take a census (elevate the heads of people)	nasa et rosh ha-anashim	נָשָׂא אֶת רֹאשׁ הָאֲנָשִׁים
to raise, elevate, pardon (lift head of so-and-so)	nasa et rosh plonee	נָשָׂא אֶת רֹאשׁ פְּלוֹנִי
behead (lift head of so-and-so from on him)	nasa et rosh plonee me-alav	נָשָׂא אֶת רֹאשׁ פְּלוֹנִי מֵעָלָיו

Hit the Trail!

and Word Study

Elevate All Donors

❝ ADONAI said to Moshe, "When you take a census of the people of Isra'el and register them, each, upon registration, is to pay a ransom for his life to ADONAI, to avoid any breakout of plague . . . ❞ —Exodus 30:11-12

K I TISA (*When you elevate*) the heads, half a shekel (similar to a silver fifty cent piece) gets collected from each male over twenty years old. Coins, not heads are counted.

A census indicates a change of status. Here the nation is being elevated for the holy service of cleansing the Land of Promise. The kofer (*ransom, half-shekel payment*) enables each individual—whether rich or poor—to be numbered in the army without incurring sin (Ex. 30:14-15). The LORD commands the census during Moshe's forty days on Sinai,

but it is not implemented until Numbers 1:3.

The whole nation contributes to a sacred cause.

Each person counted "crosses over." The kofer is a "t'rumah (*offering*) to atone for your lives" (Ex. 30:15). It is paid by one who is guilty of taking a human life in circumstances not constituting murder. Here, the soldier pays a kofer at his time of mustering, in preparation for what must follow on the battle field.

Read Ex. 38:25-26. The contributions of silver totalled over 100 talents, shaped by artisans into 100 pedestals used to elevate the mishkan (dwelling). Comment on how "lifting up the head" elevated the nation for holy service.

God-Given Tablets

> **" When he had finished speaking with Moshe on Mount Sinai, ADONAI gave him the two tablets of the testimony, tablets of stone inscribed by the finger of God. "**
>
> *—Exodus 31:18*

Finally, Moshe returns with the luchot ha-edut (*tablets of the testimony*), which are "tablets of stone inscribed by the finger of God" (Ex. 31:18). What God spoke is now etched in stone!

> ## Moshe returns after forty days, with stone tablets inscribed by the LORD.

Closure on finishing the decalog parallels the first Shabbat, "when God finished" His work and rested (Ex. 31:18, cf. Gen. 2:2-3). In fact, immediately preceding this segment come the words of v'Sham'ru (*and you shall keep,*

Ex. 31:16-17). Today, Jewish congregations sing v'Sham'ru to commemorate Shabbat as sign and a b'rit olam (*everlasting covenant*). Sabbath rest is anchored not just in the decalog, but in the creation ordinances, because God rested on the seventh day.

Now the narrative resumes, implying that God spoke to Moshe all the legislation (Ex. 25-31) during his forty-day stint on Mt. Sinai, from Shavuot to 17 Tammuz, the day of the golden calf episode (Ex. 32). The 47-verse sheni segment details the people's escapades and Moshe's reactions.

> **?** *Citing Pes. 6b ("there is no early or late in the Torah"), Rashi argues that contributions for the sanctuary were taken after Yom Kippur. Sforno thinks KI TISA summarizes events that already happened. What do you think?*

Be Present Among Us

❝ *Moshe said to* ADONAI, *"Look, you say . . . 'Make these people move on!' But you haven't let me know whom you will be sending . . . Nevertheless you have said, 'I know you by name'. . ."* ❞ —Ex. 33:12

Featuring five verses (Ex. 33:12-16) as a separate segment spotlights the climax of Moshe's intercessory work with the LORD.

Moshe takes drastic action, and then intercedes with transparent intimacy.

Time flies, then freezes. In the sheni segment, Moshe saw the gala orgy at the golden calf, smashed the God-given tablets, raised up the Levites to kill 3000 idolaters, and moved his tent (the ohel moed, *tent of meeting*) out of the camp. Now he pleads for mercy in a second forty-day period of high stakes intercession (19 Tammuz to 1 Elul).

God had promised to send an angel (Ex. 33:2), but Moshe insists upon God's personal Presence. Again and again, Moshe appeals with intimacy, strongly urging God to receive back His people. Moshe appeals repeatedly to his relationship with God. The LORD relents (Ex. 33:14), but Moshe wants the nation elevated too. Moshe won't rest—won't even leave camp—unless God leads with His Presence. Finally, God agrees to elevate the nation also (Ex. 33:17).

? *Read Ex. 33:16. Moshe contends that Yisra'el cannot be different from any other nation unless it is distinguished by God's personal Presence. How does the above verse relate to the Aleinu, sung in the liturgy of the worship service?*

Behold, the Presence!

> ❝ ADONAI *said to Moshe, "I will also do what you have asked me to do, because you have found favor in my sight, and I know you by name." But Moshe said, "I beg you to show me your glory!"* ❞ —*Ex. 33:17-18*

One hundred thirty-nine verses in the entire parashah—yet, twelve verses are highlighted in the shlishi and r'vi'i segments! Seven verses in this segment are given as much attention as an average of 24 verses in the other segments.

God's glory returns to elevate Moshe and the nation.

The LORD's agreement to dwell among Yisra'el puts the sanctuary building project back on track! Moshe's tent, recognized as the ohel moed (*tent of meeting*), will soon be absorbed into the heart of the mikdash (*place of holiness*) as the mishkan (*place of the Sh'chinah or Presence*).

Moshe pleads for a vision of God's glory. God limits his request with the words "that I show-favor to whom I show-favor; that I show-mercy to whom I show-mercy" (Ex. 33:19, Fox). Moshe cannot see God's face and live, but God will cause his goodness (an attribute, not His essence) to pass by. Then from behind, Moshe can glimpse His Glory (Ex. 33:23).

Read Romans 9:14-15, 22-23 in the light of Exodus 33:19. Do you find it anxiety producing to trust God, without prematurely judging His actions? Can you defend God's right to seem unreasonable and appear to act unreasonably?

Man-Made Tablets

" ADONAI *said to Moshe, "Cut yourself two tablets of stone like the first ones; and I will inscribe on the tablets the words that were on the first tablets, which you broke."* **"**

—*Exodus 34:1*

"You broke the first ones; you carve yourself the new ones!" Following the Tanchuma [29, 30], Rashi (on Ex. 32:7) likens the breaking of the God-given tablets to a scandal in which the erev rav (*the great conglomeration, the mixed multitude*) degenerated "and caused degeneracy in others" [Rashi, 1995, p. 450].

God investigates the matter and finds his bride's reputation unfairly impugned (cf. Gen. 39:17). But before He can clear the bride, the best friend responsible for the details of the wedding (here, Moshe) tears up the k'tubah (*marriage contract*).

When God reconciles with his wife, the best friend tells him, "Write another k'tubah for her." Replies God, "You tore it up, you buy for yourself . . . and I will write her another k'tubah in My hand" [Rashi, 1995, p. 472].

The k'tubah is rewritten, and the covenant is reconsecrated at Sinai.

Thus, Yisra'el takes a rap for the actions of 3000 idolaters, and Moshe must carve out a blank contract and redo the covenant ceremony.

? *Read Gen. 39:11-19. Stone [on Gen. 41:45; Walk GENESIS!, p. 180] says that God eventually elevated Yosef from his scandal by giving him Potifar's wife as bride. What are the parallels to Yisra'el's rap for whoring after other gods?*

164 • KI TISA   Chamishi   Exodus 34:1-9

The Nation Elevated

> **❝** *He said, "Here, I am making a covenant; in front of all your people I will do wonders such as have not been created anywhere on earth or in any nation . . ."* **❞**
> —*Exodus 34:10*

"Here, I am making a covenant . . . I will do nifla'ot (*wonders*) such as have not been created anywhere on earth or in any nation. All the people around you will see the work of ADONAI. What I am going to do through you will be nora (*awesome*)!" (Ex. 34:10).

> *God covenants to elevate Yisra'el and work wonders among the nations.*

Yisra'el is sternly enjoined to avoid the snares of sealing a covenant with Canaanites, to avoid intermarriage, and to avoid making molten images (Ex. 34:15-17). Such temptations must be summarily rejected, lest they lead to idolatry, the breaking of Yisra'el's covenant, and the stumbling of the nation (cf. Ro. 11:11).

If Yisra'el keeps herself pure from idolatry, then the LORD will dwell in her midst. He will elevate the nation with awesome works, by multiplying nifla'ot (*wonders*) that catch the attention of leaders like Pharaoh in all the nations (cf. Ex. 7:1-5; 15:11, 18). But Yisra'el must remain holy, or His Presence will not remain!

> **?** *Read Josh. 3:5, 16-17; Ex. 14:29; John 14:12-14. Believers are promised, by Yeshua, that He will answer prayer in His name, and He will do awesome works to multiply the Father's glory. Are awesome works yet to come? Explain.*

Covenant Renewed

❝ ADONAI said to Moshe, "Write these words down, because they are the terms of the covenant I have made with you and with Isra'el." ❞

—Exodus 34:27

Moshe's second forty day stay on Mount Sinai begins on the new moon of Elul and concludes on Yom Kippur [Ramban]. Again, Moshe goes forty full days without food, as he abides in the Presence of the LORD (Ex. 34:28, cf. 24:18).

The Covenant at Sinai is renewed in glory.

Reviewing the steps of history, Moshe is again charged to write the covenant rights and laws [Ex. 34:27; cf. Ex. 24:4, 7; Delitzsch, p. 243].

When Moshe returned from his first forty-day stay, there is no mention that his face shone with the light of the glory of God. Here, Aharon and the children of Yisra'el see Moshe descending from Sinai with the new set of tablets; and immediately they shrink from his radiating face (Ex. 34:30). When Moshe calls to them, Aharon returns, followed by the leaders of the assembly; only afterward do the people draw near (Ex. 34:31-32). One can say that Shavuot at Mount Sinai is renewed on Yom Kippur!

? • Compare Ex. 34:31-32 to Ex. 24:9-12. Picture Moshe, with unveiled face, teaching Torah first to Aharon; then to Aharon with his sons; then to Aharon, sons, and elders; and finally to everyone [Eruv. 54b]. Who beholds God's glory?

Glowing for God

❝ But when the people of Isra'el saw Moshe's face, that the skin of Moshe's face shone, he would put the veil back over his face until he went in again to speak with ADONAI. ❞   —Exodus 34:35

Moshe once worried that the people would not respect his office (Ex. 4:1). God replies that the people will believe the signs, and at first the people believe (Ex. 4:2-5, 28-31)!

Moshe's face radiates God's glory, as he teaches Torah from Sinai.

Eventually, the people need to see mighty deeds to renew faith in the LORD and in Moshe, His servant (Ex. 14:31). But time passes, and the people's belief must be renewed again. God proposes to speak aloud to Moshe, to bolster belief in God and also in His Moshe, His prophet (Ex. 19:9).

All too clearly, the people's belief dissolves once more, when Moshe is on the mount (Ex. 32:1). Without a continual presence and reminder, the people's belief seems to fade.

Thus, when the covenant is renewed, God elevates Moshe higher yet. Moshe alone ascends the mount, and he returns with a glorious face that must be veiled—just as the clouds veil the glory of God (Ex. 34:3, 30, 34-35)!

Read Ex. 34:34-35. With unveiled face, Moshe would speak to God and then teach the people. Explain how Moshe's unveiled face brings the Shavuot experience of Sinai directly into the life of the community.

Presence Manifested   *Meander*

" When all the people saw it, they fell on their faces and said, "ADONAI is God! ADONAI is God!" **"**

— 1 Kings 18:39

Eliyahu (*Elijah*) builds an altar in a place God chooses to make His name known. This privilege was permitted any firstborn in Yisra'el prior to the golden calf (Ex. 20:24(21 ך"נב)).

> ## God meets the people in the Land at an altar built by His prophet.

Eliyahu is called by the LORD to confront Yisra'el's headlong plunge into idolatry. Ach'av (*Ahab*) is the eighth idolatrous king to follow in the footsteps of Yarov'am (*Jeroboam*), son of N'vat, who set up molten, golden calves in high places for worship (1 Ki. 12:32-33).

Now Ach'av accelerates evil by building a temple and altar to the Phoenician god, Ba'al (1 Ki. 16:30-32). Eliyahu shuts up the sky for three years (1 Ki. 17:1; 18:1; cf. Rev. 11:3-6). Then the LORD sends him to confront Ach'av. The nation thirsts for rain! Ba'al is the storm god, and fire is his domain of command. So Eliyahu calls for an altar, a sacrifice, and a contest to see Who can send fire to consume the sacrifice and rain to end the drought!

? *Read Ex. 32:10; 1 Ki. 18:19, 40. When God's wrath is kindled against idolaters, God tells Moshe, "Now leave me alone, so that my anger can blaze . . . and I will put an end to them." What happens to the priests of Ba'al?*

...*ings* Radiating in God's Glory

> ❝ *So all of us, with faces unveiled, see as in a mirror the glory of the Lord; and we are being changed into his very image, from one degree of glory to the next, by ADONAI the Spirit.* ❞ — *2 Corinthians 3:18*

What purpose in life is greater than this? Ultimately, God cares more about who you are than what you do for Him. Who you are is determined by your maturity, which advances "from one degree of glory to the next, by ADONAI the Spirit" (2 Cor. 3:18).

The New Covenant enables believers to be changed into the image of Messiah.

In this reading, believers stand as did Moshe, when heaven descended on Sinai and he was called to the top.

Moshe spoke to God face to face, and his face radiated the glory of God. Built on "newer and better promises" (Heb. 8:5-8), the B'rit Chadashah provides for transformation.

Although the fault with people (such as weakness of the flesh) still persists, believers have direct access to God through Messiah, who has written His word on tablets of flesh (2 Cor. 3:3). We who believe can behold the glory of God. By reflecting His light as we approach Him in prayer, our hearts are irradiated with the image of Messiah Himself!

> **?** There's a story about a man who died of thirst in a bath tub. Water, water everywhere and not a drop to drink!
> ● The man didn't drink because he knew he had no glass! What blinds you from reflecting the light of God's glory?

Talk Your Walk . . .

A mini-review of all history takes place in KI TISA (*when you elevate*). Three forty-day periods characterize the time from Shavuot through summer to Yom Kippur. The first forty days, God elevates the nation to the service of cleansing the Land of Promise from accursed idolaters. A kofer (*ransom*) is taken from each person elevated to service in the LORD's army. It is the first step in redeeming the

> *The nation is set apart for holy service to God.*

Land and setting up a pattern to redeem all nations of the world.

Moshe returns with the God-given tablets. But the nation has already broken the first two commands spoken at Sinai. In a fury, Moshe shatters the very same words carved by God Himself onto the stone! He orders a cleansing of the camp, and the Levites kill 3000 idolaters in a single day.

During the second forty-day period, Moshe moves his tent out of the camp, a self-imposed exile. God meets with Moshe at the door of his tent, now called the ohel moed (*tent of meeting*). The people watch and wait in sorrow. Moshe intercedes, offering his life for the people. God forgives and agrees, once more, to dwell with visible Presence among them.

In the third period, Moshe spends another forty days at Sinai's summit, in the clouds of heaven and the Presence of the LORD. The covenant is renewed, and Moshe returns—glowing—with tablets in hand.

Oasis

... Walk Your Talk

The divine purpose of history is to restore man, step by step, to Gan Eden. Man must be elevated from the fall, a consequence of disobedience. When God was visible, He cloaked His Presence in the midst of a cloud. The children of Yisra'el got used to the cloud and the manna in the same way that you have grown accustomed to airplanes, telephones, e-mail, and, for that matter, answers to prayer!

Yet Moshe actually rested with God on the seventh Shabbat after the exodus from Egypt. He disappeared into heavenly clouds and learned Torah, taught personally by God in His heavenly abode on earth. And God taught Moshe exactly how to make a heavenly copy of the celestial dwelling on earth. Make no mistake about it, God is perfectly serious about bringing heaven down to earth. What is written in the closing chapters of Revelation first began at Sinai. Earth will be redeemed and transformed, before a new creation descends. Your physical body must be redeemed and trans-

> *Spiritual transformation starts with dwelling in the Presence of God.*

formed, too! But you must set aside time now—to gaze on the Presence of God, to irradiate His Presence, to change your spiritual tastes, and to be transformed from image to image into the glory of His son.

 Shabbat Shalom!

ויקהל Moshe,
assembling Israelites
to build God's dwelling
and light the nights.
"Bring those offerings
for God's delight
to B'tsal'el, the craftsman,
a Y'hudah-ite!"

So day after day,
the gifts piled high—
gold, silver, bronze, linens,
and wood to the sky!
"Dayenu! Enough!"
you could hear Moshe sigh,
as we all built community
with God in our eye!

Walk VAYAKHEL!
35:1-38:20

וַיַּקְהֵל

And he assembled

TORAH—Exodus 35:1-38:20
  1st Assemble the Assembly!—Exodus 35:1
  2nd Heartfelt Gifts—Exodus 35:21
  3rd Spirit-Filled Workmanship—Exodus 35:30-31a
  4th Construction Begins—Exodus 36:8
  5th Construction Continues—Exodus 36:20
  6th Furniture—Exodus 37:17
  7th The Courtyard—Exodus 38:1
  Maftir Finishing the Work—Exodus 38:20

HAFTARAH—1 Kings 7:13-26, 40-50
  Pure Gold—1 Kings 7:50

B'RIT CHADASHAH—Hebrews 9:1-10
  The Limits of Pure Gold—Hebrews 9:8, 10b

Assemble for Assembly Time

◄ Looking Back

B'REISHEET (*in the beginning*) God created Gan Eden and placed Adam there to be present with Him. Adam disobeys, but men like Avraham walk with God. God's Presence accompanies his grandson Ya'akov into exile and remains with him. VAY'CHI Ya'akov (*and Jacob lived*) through his sons.

Exodus begins: these are the SH'MOT (*names*) of Ya'akov's sons, reunited in Egypt as a nation-in-embryo. Pharaoh oppresses them to curb their growth. VA'ERA (*and I appeared*), says the LORD, to make good on My promises to Avraham. God tells Moshe, BO (*enter!*) and negotiate to free the sons of Yisra'el. B'SHALACH Par'oh (*when Pharaoh let go*), God leads Yisra'el with His Presence. YITRO (*Jethro*) reunites Moshe's family. The LORD covenants with Yisra'el. The nation must be ruled by God's MISHPATIM (*judgments*).

These are the SH'MOT
of sons oppressed in Egypt.
Yet God assures Moshe:
VA'ERA . . . *now* BO *to Pharaoh!*
B'SHALACH, *God brings us out.*
YITRO *advises:*
Appoint judges to use God's
MISHPATIM.
God tells Moshe:
Take T'RUMAH *from the heart,*
and T'TSAVEH *My people*
to keep the light burning all night.
KI TISA *to holy service,*
follow God to the top!
VAYAKHEL—*and Moshe assembled*
all the community
to build God's Dwelling!

On the mount, God tells Moshe to take T'RUMAH (*offering*) to elevate the nation and build Him a dwelling. He adds, T'TSAVEH (*you shall command*) Yisra'el to keep a holy fire burning at night.

Log

Next, God orders a census: **KI TISA** (*when you elevate*) the nation to take the Land, elevate the army. The whole nation will gladly contribute to the sacred cause.

While Moshe is gone for forty days, the people panic and make a molten calf. Moshe returns, with stone tablets in hand. He sees the idol and smashes the tablets. Moshe takes drastic action, ordaining the Levites by sword to slay the idolaters.

Then Moshe removes his tent from the camp and intercedes for another forty days. God finally relents and forgives the people. Once more, Moshe scales the mountain for yet another forty days. This time, God tells him to write the stone tablets himself. God's glory returns; Moshe glows from the encounter.

In VAYAKHEL . . .

The Key People are Moshe (*Moses*), all the congregation, B'tsal'el (*Bezalel*), Oholi'av (*Oholiab*), and gifted artisans.

The Scene is the wilderness.

Main Events include Moshe telling the words God has commanded—to keep Shabbat, take offerings, make the dwelling; offerings brought; B'tsal'el and Oholi'av filled with God's Spirit; offerings stopped, enough collected; artisans make curtains, bars, veil, screen, ark, poles, cherubim, table, rings, poles, lampstand, lamps, incense altar, holy anointing oil, incense, altar of burnt offering with horns, utensils, poles, laver, court, linen hangings, pillars, sockets, screen for gate, etc.

VAYAKHEL Moshe (*and Moses assembled*) the community to build God a dwelling, so that God goes before His people to the Land of C'na'an . . .

The Trail Ahead

The Path

ויקהל משה
את כל עדת בני ישראל
ויאמר אלהם אלה הדברים
אשר צוה יהוה לעשת אתם

—שמות לה/א

letter:	ל	הֶ	קְ	יַ	וַ
letter:	lahmed	hay	koof	yod	vav
sound:	L	**Hei**	K	Yyah	Vah

and he assembled = VAYAKHEL = ויקהל

Work

The Legend

and assembled	*va-yakhel*	וַיַּקְהֵל
Moses	*Mosheh*	מֹשֶׁה
— all the congregation of	*et-kol-adat*	אֶת־כָּל־עֲדַת
sons of Israel	*b'nei Yisra'el*	בְּנֵי יִשְׂרָאֵל
and said	*va-yomer*	וַיֹּאמֶר
unto them	*alehem*	אֲלֵהֶם
these (are) the words	*eleh ha-d'varim*	אֵלֶּה הַדְּבָרִים
that commanded	*asher-tsivah*	אֲשֶׁר־צִוָּה
the LORD	*ADONAI*	יְהֹוָה
to do them	*la'asot otam*	לַעֲשֹׂת אֹתָם׃

—Exodus 35:1

Related Words

assembly, congregation (Neh. 5:7, Dt. 33:4)	*k'hilah*	קְהִלָּה
speaker in an assembly (Eccl. 1:1-2)	*kohehlet*	קֹהֶלֶת
assembly (Ps. 26:12)	*makhale*	מַקְהֵל
crowd, gathering	*kahahl*	קָהָל
choir, chorus, assembly	*makhelah*	מַקְהֵלָה

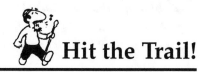

Hit the Trail!

Assemble the Assembly!

" Moshe assembled the whole community of the people of Isra'el and said to them, "These are the things which ADONAI has ordered you to do." "

—Exodus 35:1

Now assembled, we move together by the command of the LORD, "These are the things which ADONAI has ordered you to do" (Ex. 35:1, 10-11).

Construction of the sanctuary redeems the sin of the golden calf.

The actual construction of the mishkan (*sanctuary*) is described—step by step—in startling contrast to the incident of the golden calf, when the people vayikahel (*assembled to demand*) "gods to go ahead of us" (Ex.32:1). At the golden calf, the people "broke off" earrings of gold, but here individuals give a t'rumah (*offering*) joyfully, according to "whose heart makes him willing" (Ex. 35:5). In this way, a redemptive assembling of the community around the building of the mishkan provides a rallying ground for the people to repent making the molten image of a golden calf.

Spiritually, the people assemble together as a living k'hilah (*community*) with the God-given hope that the LORD Himself will dwell among them (Ex. 6:7; 25:8; 33:16).

? Read Ex. 34:32. According to Sforno, the LORD commands building the sanctuary. He interprets the command to ● observe Shabbat (Ex. 35:2) to apply during the building of the sanctuary. Which command is more important?

Heartfelt Gifts

❝ and they came, everyone whose heart stirred him and everyone whose spirit made him willing, and brought ADONAI's *offering for the work on the tent of meeting, for the service in it and for the holy garments.* ❞ —Ex. 35:21

Only those with hearts that "stirred" or spirits that made them "willing" could bring t'rumah (an elevation *offering*) for the skilled work of the ohel moed (*tent of meeting*).

God did not want to build a dwelling and thus elevate the nation, if such a project were based on anything other than heartfelt gifts! The people respond with a picture of ecstasy-in-action. Women dig into their dowries (for some, their only security) and come with their fathers and husbands to give gold from their bracelets, earrings, necklaces, signet rings, and body ornaments (Ex. 35:22).

All the people give their very best gifts, straight from the heart!

So effusive is the outpouring of gifts that Torah later tells us that the craftsmen stopped work to ask Moshe to order a halt to the t'rumot (Ex. 36:4-7). Every segment of society contributed. Last, but not least to give, the leaders contribute the rare stones, spices, and oils for anointing and for light (Ex. 35:27-29).

? *Read Ex. 35:20-21. First Moshe gives the order for the people to bring thirteen specified items that qualify as t'rumot (offerings) for the* LORD's *dwelling. Explain who exits (v. 20) and who returns (v. 21). What is Torah saying?*

Spirit-Filled Workmanship

> ❝ *Moshe said to the people of Isra'el, "See, Adonai has singled out B'tzal'el the son of Uri, the son of Hur, of the tribe of Y'hudah. He has filled him with the Spirit of God . . ."* ❞
> —*Exodus 35:30-31a*

Remember that Aharon and Hur were in charge when Moshe ascended Mount Sinai to receive the God-given tablets (Ex. 24:14). Tradition says that Hur was murdered for opposing the making of the golden calf [Stone on Ex. 32:6, p. 495].

> *The LORD calls B'tsal'el to the spirit-filled creativity of making the sanctuary.*

Now, Hur's grandson is elevated to master architect and craftsman of the sanctuary project (Ex. 31:2). The text literally reads, "See! The LORD

called by name B'tsal'el, son of Uri, son of Hur" (Ex. 35:31). It is unusual to mention the names of both a father and grandfather; but here, Hur's grandson molds the gold of the k'hilah into a dwelling for the living God! Hur's life is redeemed in the work of his grandson, who fashions gold to elevate the nation! B'tsal'el's spirit-filled work on God's dwelling parallels God's work during the first six days (Gen. 2:2). B'chol m'la'chah (*in all creative activity*), B'tsal'el is equipped to build the sanctuary (Ex. 35:31).

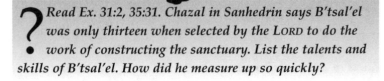

> ❓ *Read Ex. 31:2, 35:31. Chazal in Sanhedrin says B'tsal'el was only thirteen when selected by the LORD to do the work of constructing the sanctuary. List the talents and skills of B'tsal'el. How did he measure up so quickly?*

Construction Begins

" All the skilled men among them who did the work made the tabernacle, using ten sheets of finely woven linen and of blue, purple and scarlet yarn. He made them with k'ruvim worked in . . . " —Exodus 36:8

Actual construction begins, starting with the ma'aseh choshev (*woven design*) of the k'ruvim (*cherubs*) (Ex. 36:8). The orders given in Parashat T'RUMAH (specifically, Ex. 26:1-37) are carried out, almost verbatim! But this portion is centered around construction; so set-up commands, such as joining tapestries to boards, are omitted (Ex. 36:18-19; cf. Ex. 26:11-14).

Tradition describes the woven design in all its complexity [Yoma 72b]. K'ruvim appear as lions on one side and as eagles on the other side of the curtain [Rashi].

Make curtains for the resting place of God's Presence.

Over the weaving (Ex. 36:8-13) rests a protective covering of black goat's hair (also called "the tent over the mishkan"), and then the waterproof covers of hides and skins (Ex. 36:14-19). When the nation encamps, the Sh'chinah (*Presence*) of the LORD actually rests upon these magnificent curtains.

> *Read Ex. 26:9b, 11, and compare with Ex. 36:16, 18. Explain the reason for the omission of these details from*
> • *Ex. 26. P'KUDEI has a section devoted to erecting the mishkan. Would you expect to find the omissions there?*

Construction Continues

“ *He made the upright planks of acacia-wood for the tabernacle.* **”**

—*Exodus 36:20*

Beams for the frame of the mishkan (*dwelling*) stand 15 feet by 2.75 feet. Each beam is doubled with pegs that connect the beams at the top and bottom.

Artisans construct the frame for the tent.

The reading becomes tedious, as precise details are spelled out for each respective side of the frame. Speaking generally, a total of 50 boards and 100 silver pedestals supports the mishkan's frame. The silver for the pedestals is drawn from the half-shekels that all Yisra'el contributed at the census count. Curiously, KI TISA (*when you elevate*) all Yisra'el (Ex. 30:12), then their T'RUMAH (*offering*) physically elevates the celestial tent upon which ADONAI's Sh'chinah (*Presence*) rests.

This arrangement of upright boards, doubled and attached to twin pedestals, closely resembles the celestial abode of the Canaanite deity, El [Cassuto, p. 323]. Small wonder that seeing a celestial abode in Yisra'el's midst terrified the Canaanites!

? *Read Ex. 25:8-9; 26:30. Recall that heaven descended on Mount Sinai, and God showed Moshe the design for His earthly abode. In what way does the mishkan portray a place where heaven meets earth?*

Furniture

> **"** He made the menorah of pure gold. He made it of hammered work; its base, shaft, cups, rings of outer leaves and flowers were a single unit. **"**
>
> —*Exodus 37:17*

Gold covers both the m'norah and the incense altar. The m'norah was made from a single ingot of gold weighing a kikar (*talent*, perhaps 66 pounds, Ex. 37:24).

First the sanctuary is constructed, then its furniture.

An exquisite work, the m'norah was hammered—its shaft, stem, goblets, knobs, and blossoms resembled a budding almond, the first plant to blossom in the spring. Descriptions in the segment here parallel those which the LORD commanded Moshe (Ex. 37:17-24; cf. Ex. 25:31-40). Once again, omitted details refer to the placement of the m'norah in the structure—a question relating to erecting the sanctuary, not to constructing it.

The exact dimensions of the m'norah are not given—only its weight and composite unity, based on its being carefully hammered from one ingot of gold.

It is noteworthy that as one approaches the Holy of Holies, all furniture is overlaid with gold, gold in abundance!

? *Explain why Ex. 25:37, 30:1-5 are detailed in Ex. 40:25, 26-27. Comment on why these details are omitted from the accounts of the construction of the lampstand (Ex. 37:17-24) and the altar of incense (Ex. 37:25-29).*

The Courtyard

❝ He made the altar for burnt offerings of acacia-wood, seven-and-a-half feet long and seven-and-a-half feet wide—it was square—and four-and-a-half feet high. ❞
                                                    —*Exodus 38:1*

ommands given in Exodus 27 are now carried out almost word for word in Exodus 38. VAYAKHEL Moshe (*and Moses assembled*) what the people gave as a T'RUMAH (*offering*).

Building the courtyard completes construction of the LORD's dwelling.

Construction starts with the copper altar near the center of the courtyard (Ex. 38:1-7, cf. Ex. 27:1-8) and concludes with the fence surrounding the courtyard (Ex. 38:9-20, cf. Ex. 27:9-19). Also, the bronze wash basin is constructed (Ex. 38:8, cf. Ex. 30:18).

Once the mishkan is operational, those entering the courtyard area must be ritually clean, exactly as the LORD required at Sinai (Ex. 19:10-15, Lev. 15:31-34). The courtyard is holy: "Through all your generations this is to be the olat tamid (*regular burnt offering*) at the entrance to the tent of meeting before ADONAI. There is where I will meet with you to speak with you" (Ex. 29:42). The courtyard surrounds the Holy Place where the LORD speaks.

? • Read Ex. 27:3, 30:17-21, 27:18. Explain why these details about the priests are omitted in the present segment about construction. Also, discuss whether God speaks at the copper altar, outside the door of the tent (cf. Ex. 33:7-11).

Finishing the Work

> ❝ *The tent pegs for the tabernacle and for the courtyard around it were of bronze.* ❞
>
> —*Exodus 38:20*

Outermost details for finishing the construction of the mishkan (*dwelling*) and the precincts of its courtyard are spelled out, right down to the very last bronze tent peg!

Torah enumerates the very last details of constructing the sanctuary.

The work of ministry can be mundane [a word Webster's dictionary describes as "characterized by the practical, transitory, and ordinary: having no concern for the ideal or the heavenly," p. 557].

Ironically, the exact opposite reality is transpiring. The driving of the final tent peg touches upon a dream of Avraham, who tented the perimeter of the Land and staked his claim in faith (Gen. 12:8, 13:3, 18; 18:1; Heb. 11:8-9). Now, the sons of Avraham are en route to the Land. The LORD has commanded construction of a celestial abode upon which He rests His very Presence, and the details of constructing this mishkan are fulfilled, right down to the very last bronze tent peg! The dream goes full circle!

> *Think of a mundane time in your life when you have been faithful to God's call upon you, right down to the very last detail. As you stake your claim of faith, based upon obedience without expectation, what happens?*

Pure Gold

Meander

" *. . . and the hinges of gold, both those for the doors of the inner house, the Especially Holy Place, and those for the doors of the house, that is, of the temple.* **"**
—1 Kings 7:50

Hiram finishes the work of building the LORD's dwelling in Y'rushalayim. The account follows the form of archival records, and in fact ends with words mirroring God's creative activity on day six of the creation account ("So Hiram finished all the work," 1 Ki. 7:40b, JPS).

> *Construct the temple from the purest of gold.*

Hiram, like B'tsal'el, is commissioned to represent his people (2 Chr. 2:12-13 (13-14

תנ"ך), cf. Ex. 31:2-5). Indeed, he is "filled" with wisdom for the appointed task (1 Ki. 7:14, cf. Ex. 36:1).

Interestingly, the Haftarah halts abruptly, just before verse 51, when King David's gold, the spoils of war, is added to the temple treasury. Seized gold is not used in the temple. Rather, the temple is constructed solely from pure gold of the t'rumot (elevation *offerings)* of King Solomon. Like the mishkan which preceded it, this temple houses a holy God who dwells amidst only the purest of offerings.

? *Read Ex. 32:3-4, 20; 35:5, 20, 22; 1 Ki. 7:48-51. Explain the reasons why God excluded the gold from the golden calf and from David in building vessels for the Most Holy Place? What is your purest offering, that you can give God?*

> **"** By this arrangement, the Ruach HaKodesh showed that . . . the way into the Holiest Place was still closed. . . until the time for God to reshape the whole structure.**"**
>   —Hebrews 9:8, 10b

In effect, the mishkan introduced a system of barriers (Heb. 9:2-5) which limited the access of worshippers to the Sh'chinah (*Presence*).

> ### The earthly sanctuary limits direct access to God.

Only priests could enter the Holy Place (Heb. 9:6), and only the Kohen Gadol (*High Priest*) could enter the Most Holy Place—and that was only once a year, subject to formal ritual procedures. Blood is always required to effect cleansing (Lev. 16:15-16)

in order to enter the Most Holy Place (Heb. 9:7).

The author of Hebrews comments that this arrangement shows that the way into the mishkan (*dwelling*) in heaven had not yet been disclosed (Heb. 9:8).

Thus, direct access to God was not available, and approaching God could take place only through chosen representatives, the kohanim and the Kohen Gadol (*priests* and *High Priest*). God would have to "reshape the whole structure" to open up direct access to His glorious Presence (Heb. 9:10).

? *Read Hebrews 9:7. Explain why blood entry was always required, when the Kohen Gadol entered the Most Holy Place. What is Ruach HaKodesh really telling us about entering the holy ground of God's abiding Presence?*

Talk Your Walk . . .

Assembling the community, Moshe relates God's command to gather t'rumah (an elevation *offering*) from those who are moved, spiritually, to contribute. Gathering gifts brings the community together, as does building the building upon which the Presence of the LORD will rest. Only heartfelt gifts are accepted, by divine fiat. Gifts pour in; within days, the artisans ask Moshe to order a halt!

God elevates B'tsal'el, grandson of Chur (*Hur*), to mold the gold into the exact likeness of the furniture revealed to Moshe on the summit of Sinai. Earrings of gold donated to mold a golden calf (Talmud says at the cost of Chur's life) are now superceded by earrings of gold offered to mold the golden altar, the kapporet (*ark cover*), and the k'ruvim (*cherubim*) that guard the way to the Presence of the LORD. The spiritual path to Gan Eden opens!

Hopes for re-entering God's Presence, seen by Moshe from afar on Sinai, are carved out by the spirit-filled creativity of artisans under the oversight of B'tsal'el (*Shadow of God*) and Oholi'av (*Tent of the Father*). Curtains woven with k'ruvim become the resting place for God's visible Presence. The sanctuary, then its furniture, is constructed, detail by detail. Building the courtyard completes all the work. It remains for the nation to enter into God's rest on the seventh day!

> *Repentance achieved, the nation constructs a dwelling for the LORD.*

Oasis

. . . Walk Your Talk

W hen man first disobeyed the command of the LORD, he was driven from Gan Eden, lest he eat from Etz haChayim (*the Tree of Life*) and live forever. In man's twisted state of disobedience, such an act would frustrate God's purposes for man. Accordingly, God drove man from Gan Eden and stationed k'ruvim (*cherubim*) to guard the path to eternal life.

Now, God promises His visible Presence to a nation redeemed from bondage and exile. The way back into the Presence of God is opened a crack. A spiritual path from exile back to the entrance to Gan Eden is built by spirit-filled artisans, raised up for the task. The nation is elevated for its priestly calling to lead all nations to worship the LORD, and Him alone.

Spiritually, the way is open for you to enter the Presence of God through prayer with eyes of faith. Spiritually, you can reflect upon God with eyes of faith and hopes shaped by God's plan of redemption. Your life is trans-

> *Cultivate Messiah's tastes for fellowship with God.*

formed supernaturally, when you spiritually nourish yourself with the hopes and promises of God. Will you cultivate a taste for God?

Shabbat Shalom!

פְקוּדֵי "accounts for"
materials used,
so nobody would say
that the gifts were abused.
People gave silver
and copper and gold.
Artisans wove patterns
for worship so bold.

We set up the Tent
for haShem to dwell,
made the High Priest's robe
with many a bell,
lit the lamps, burnt the incense
(a very sweet smell),
and beheld God's glory
as the Ruach fell!

Walk P'KUDEI!
38:21-40:38

Accountings of

TORAH—Exodus 38:21-40:38

HAFTARAH—1 Kings 7:51-8:21

B'RIT CHADASHAH—Hebrews 8:1-13

Accountings of
Spirit-Filled Service

Hiker's

◀ Looking Back

B'REISHEET (*in the beginning*), God created Gan Eden (*Garden of Eden, paradise*). He made man in His image to be fruitful, order creation, and rule over it. Adam chooses to disobey. Soon his firstborn, Kayin, succumbs to sibling rivalry, gets cursed, and is driven from the presence of the LORD. God judges Kayin and his sons. In contrast Noach, then Avraham and son, walk in covenant blessings. God's Presence guides Ya'akov into exile, first to Charan, later to Egypt.

Exodus begins: and these are the SH'MOT (*names*) of Ya'akov's sons, the family that unites in exile, as a nation-in-embryo. God blesses Yisra'el's sons to be fruitful. They multiply exceedingly, fill Goshen, and threaten Egypt. Pharaoh uses slavery to oppress them.

These are the SH'MOT of sons enslaved. God keeps His covenant: VA'ERA . . . now BO to Pharaoh! B'SHALACH, our exodus begins. YITRO advises Moshe to appoint judges to govern by God's MISHPATIM. God instructs: Take T'RUMAH, and T'TSAVEH My people to let the light shine. KI TISA to holy service, follow God to the top. VAYAKHEL Moshe everyone to build the tabernacle, so God might dwell among us. These are P'KUDEI—accountings of the Sh'chinah glory of the LORD!

VA'ERA (*and I appeared*), says the LORD, to make good on My promises to Avraham to free the nation. God tells Moshe, BO (*enter!*) and negotiate with Pharaoh. God punishes Pharaoh, measure for measure. B'SHALACH Par'oh (*when Pharaoh let go*), God leads guides the sons of Yisra'el with His Presence.

Log

Near Sinai, **YITRO** (*Jethro*) reunites Moshe's family. He advises Moshe to appoint a judiciary to determine case law using God's **MISHPATIM** (*judgments*). Then at Sinai, God speaks!

On the mount, God tells Moshe to take a collective **T'RUMAH** (*offering*) to elevate the nation and build a dwelling for His Presence. The LORD adds, **T'TSAVEH** (*you shall command*) Yisra'el to light the lights in the Holy Place at nights. God tells Moshe, **KI TISA** (*when you elevate*) the nation to a sacred cause, idols will fall. Yisra'el repents idolatry. Moshe rewrites the tablets and glows from being in God's Presence.

VAYAKHEL (*and he assembled*) the people to build the dwelling. When the work was finished, **P'KUDEI** (*accountings of*) materials were

In P'KUDEI . . .

The Key People are Moshe (*Moses*), the Levites, Itamar (*Ithamar*), B'tsal'el (*Bezalel*), Oholi'av (*Oholiab*), the Israelites, Aharon (*Aaron*) and sons.

The Scene is the wilderness of Sinai.

Main Events include inventory of tabernacle materials; priest's garments, according to LORD's commands; Moshe blessing people; God ordering the tabernacle set-up, arrangement of furnishings, and consecration; instructions for priests to wash, dress, and be anointed; Moshe raising tabernacle on 1st day 1st month of 2nd year; lamps lit, incense burnt, offerings made for worship; laver set up for washing; all work finished, cloud covering tabernacle, glory of the LORD filling it; and cloud/fire guiding Yisra'el throughout journeys.

reported. Then God radiates the dwelling with the glory of His Presence . . .

The Trail Ahead

Compass

The Path

אֵלֶּה פְקוּדֵי הַמִּשְׁכָּן
מִשְׁכַּן הָעֵדֻת
אֲשֶׁר פֻּקַּד עַל פִּי מֹשֶׁה
עֲבֹדַת הַלְוִיִּם
בְּיַד אִיתָמָר בֶּן אַהֲרֹן הַכֹּהֵן

—שמות לח/כא

פְּ	ק	ו	דֵ	י
letter: pay	koof	vav	dalet	yod
sound: P'	K	OO	**Dei**	EE

accountings of = **P'KUDEI** = פְקוּדֵי

Work

The Legend

these (are) <u>accountings of</u>	eleh <u>f'kudei</u>	אֵלֶּה פְקוּדֵי
the tabernacle	ha-mishkan	הַמִּשְׁכָּן
tabernacle of the testimony	mishkan ha-edoot	מִשְׁכַּן הָעֵדֻת
that were counted	asher pookad	אֲשֶׁר פֻּקַד
by mouth of Moses	al-pee Mosheh	עַל־פִּי מֹשֶׁה
work of the Levites	avodat ha-L'viyim	עֲבֹדַת הַלְוִיִּם
by hand of Ithamar	b'yad Itamar	בְּיַד אִיתָמָר
son of Aaron	ben-Aharon	בֶּן־אַהֲרֹן
the priest	ha-kohen	הַכֹּהֵן׃

—*Exodus 38:21*

Related Words

to order, command, enumerate, count, number, review	pakad	פָּקַד
clerk	pakeed	פָּקִיד
bureaucratic	p'kidooti	פְּקִידוּתִי
deposit, pledge	pikadohn	פִּקָדוֹן
Book of Numbers (Note: the name below is more common)	chumash ha-pikudeem	חֻמַּשׁ הַפְּקוּדִים
Book of Numbers ("in wilderness of")	b'midbar	בְּמִדְבַּר

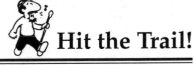

Hit the Trail!

Final Accounting

" *These are the accounts of the tabernacle, the tabernacle of the testimony, recorded, as Moshe ordered, by the L'vi'im under the direction of Itamar the son of Aharon, the cohen.* " —Exodus 38:21

P'KUDEI records *accountings* for materials used in the construction of the tabernacle. The accounts were kept by Itamar, the chief auditor. B'tsal'el and Oholi'av provided the figures. Moshe ordered the audit—most probably to stay above reproach, even though people trusted him.

Moshe orders an audit of the congregation's accounts.

In all, 2800 pounds of gold, 9600 pounds of silver, and 6700 pounds of copper were collected and used. These quantities will vary according to one's assumptions of the weight of a talent. The quantities of precious metals used may seem large, until one discovers that Alexander the Great found 400 times this amount of gold at Susa and 1200 times this amount at Persepolis!

The segment ends with words of accountability between the people and the LORD: everything was carried out ka'asher tsivah ADONAI et Moshe (*as ADONAI ordered Moshe,* Ex. 39:1).

? *Even the most trusted of God's servants requires accountability. And the humble, like Moshe, will require it of themselves. Read Phil. 2:3-4, 1 Tim. 3:7. Search yourself. To whom are you accountable in important things?*

Priestly Vestments

> " He made the ritual vest of gold, of blue, purple and scarlet yarn, and of finely woven linen. "
>
> —Exodus 39:2

Every segment except the shvi'i ends with words of accountability, the obedience of Yisra'el to the command of God ka'asher tsivah ADONAI et Moshe (*exactly as the LORD commanded Moshe*, Ex. 39:1, 21, 32, 43; 40:16, 27).

God's command to make the ephod (Ex. 39:2-7) was first spoken to Moshe (Ex. 28:6-12). Except for minor style variations, the words of the command are repeated as they are implemented. However, an occasional detail specific to implementing the command is added. For example,

Ex. 39:3 describes the actual technique of weaving gold thread into the woolen and linen threads of the ephod.

Exacting details describe how to brocade gold, woolens, and fine linen.

First the gold is rolled into sheets, hammered until it is flattened into pachim (*thin leaves*); then it is cut into fine, wire-like threads. The gold threads are brocaded or interwoven into the woolens and finely woven linen, all according to the command of the LORD to Moshe (Ex. 39:2-3, 5).

? *Read Ex. 38:22; 39:1, 5, 7, 21. What do these statements have in common? Nineteen instances in parashat P'KUDEI express the idea of exacting obedience. Explain why accountability in a life of ministry is so critical to the LORD.*

Finishing the Vestments

" He made the robe for the ritual vest; it was woven entirely of blue, with its opening in the middle, like that of a coat of mail, and with a border around the opening, so that it wouldn't tear. " —Ex. 39:22-23

Eight garments are distinctive to the Kohen Gadol (*High Priest*). The ephod and breastplate were described in the previous segment. Here, the making of the m'il (*overcoat*, Ex. 39:27), turban, caps, breeches, (v. 28), belt or sash (v. 29), and headplate (v. 30) is described.

The artisans finish the fine woven work on the priestly garments.

All items are made "as ADONAI ordered Moshe" (Ex. 39:26, 29, 31). Exacting obedience to previous instructions is marvelous to behold (see Ex. 28:31-34, 40, 42, 36-38). Only previous commands describing the order of service and consecration of priests are omitted from the present account (see Ex. 28:41, 43).

Tradition says the mishkan (*tabernacle*) was completed on 25 Kislev (in later times, the beginning of Chanukkah). A phrase recalling the creation account ends the segment, "Thus all the work . . . was finished, with the people of Isra'el doing everything exactly as ADONAI had ordered Moshe" (Ex. 39:32).

? Compare Ex. 39:32 with Gen. 6:22, which describes construction of Noach's ark. Both accounts conclude, k'chol asher tsivah . . . ken asu/asah (according to all God commanded . . . thus they/he did)! Explain the comparison.

All Parts Complete

> **" Then they brought the tabernacle to Moshe—the tent and all its furnishings, clasps, planks, crossbars, posts and sockets . . . "**
>
> —*Exodus 39:33*

Sabbath themes of the account B'REISHEET(*in the beginning*) halo this fourth segment, including a climactic finale where Yisra'el chooses to obey, finishes the work of this new creation, and pleases the LORD.

Yisra'el co-partners with God in making a new creation.

All the individual parts of the dwelling are brought to Moshe. Torah reviews a highly detailed account of each item constructed, from the Most Holy Place to packing cloths, and from the tent to its pegs. The cords for securing the tent are not mentioned in the specific commands given earlier (Ex. 35:18, cf. Ex. 27:9-18). Once again, the specific focus on items pertinent to construction stands out in this portion.

All the work of construction is completed k'chol ka'asher tsivah ADONAI et-Moshe; ken asu b'nei yisra'el et-kol-ha'avodah (*according to all that the LORD commanded Moshe, thus the children of Yisra'el finished all the work*, Ex. 39:42). Moshe imitates God. He sees the work and blesses Yisra'el.

Read Ex. 39:43, cf. Gen. 1:31, 2:3. The segment concludes that Moshe "saw" all the work; and behold, they had done the work as commanded, and Moshe blessed them. Explain how this account parallels day six of creation.

Order to Set Up

❝ *ADONAI said to Moshe, "On the first day of the first month, you are to set up the tabernacle, the tent of meeting."* ❞

—Exodus 40:1

Thus begins a new epoch in Yisra'el's service to the LORD. Yisra'el first departed Egypt on the full moon in Nisan, and now the civil year begins with freedom on the new moon, 1 Nisan.

The LORD gives the order to erect the sanctuary.

The LORD orders Moshe to set up the mishkan (*dwelling*). Commands first given Moshe on Sinai, starting with the most important item, the Ark, are repeated once more. The Ark, soon to house the Tablets, is called the Aron haEdut (*the Ark of the Testimony*, Ex. 40:3,

cf. Ex. 26:33). Further commands include  positioning all inside furniture and the screen, the outside furniture and its screen, and the priestly vestments.

God gives additional commands, pertinent solely to erecting the tabernacle, such as the command to anoint furniture or immerse/anoint priests (Ex. 40:9, cf. Ex. 30:22-30; Ex. 40:12-15). Torah states emphatically that Moshe did so, k'chol asher tsivah ADONAI oto, ken asah (*as all that commanded the LORD him, yes he did*, Ex. 40:16).

❓ *Read Ex. 40:16. Yisra'el's exacting obedience contrasts sharply with the picture of man's disobedience and failure to enter Shabbat rest with God in Gan Eden. Explain how building the mishkan transforms this picture.*

The Mishkan Raised

> " On the first day of the first month of the second year, the tabernacle was set up. "
>
> —*Exodus 40:17*

The command previously given (Ex. 40:2) is now implemented on the exact day (Ex. 40:17). Fox [p. 484] observes that for each paragraph describing the erection of the mishkan, the theme of "exact obedience" is punctuated by the words ka'asher tsivah ADONAI et Moshe (*just as the LORD commanded Moshe*, Ex. 40:19, 21, 23, 25, 27, 29, 32). The seven acts of erecting the mishkan parallel the seven days of creation—only this time even day seven goes according to what is "good" in the sight of the LORD.

At Shirat haYam (*the Song of the Sea*, Ex. 15), Yisra'el crosses into freedom, led by God's Presence in the cloud; on the scroll, the words of Torah spill poetically across the divider that sets off one column from another.

Erecting the mishkan finishes the new creation.

The idea of man's exacting obedience spills over the shishi and enters the shvi'i segment, as if to show that man enters the beginning of a new day seven with God dwelling among us!

? One walks with God today to be with Him tomorrow! Read Ex. 40:33, "Thus Moshe finished all the work."
• Comment on how finishing the work of creation parallels pounding the last tent peg.

The Final Curtain

❝ He set up the screen at the entrance to the tabernacle. ❞

—*Exodus 40:28*

Placing the final curtain as the entrance of the mishkan and setting the copper altar outside, Moshe first offers a tamid (*continual* offering, Ex. 40:28-29; cf. Ex. 29:38-42).

> ## Moshe finishes all the work God commanded.

As noted previously, each paragraph concludes with the words, ka'asher tsivah ADONAI et Moshe (*as the LORD commanded Moshe).* Cassuto notes [p. 481-483] the seven stages: erecting the mishkan (Ex.

40:18), placing the tablets in the ark (Ex. 40:20), the table (Ex. 40:22), the lampstand (Ex. 40:24), the incense altar (Ex. 40:26), the curtain and copper altar (Ex. 40:28-29), and seventh, placing the basin for washing (Ex. 40:30).

It is noteworthy that the above account closes with the words "va-y'chal Moshe et-ha-m'lachah (*and Moshe finished all the work,"* Ex. 40:33; cf. Gen. 2:1-3). M'lachah refers to planned *work* that God ceased from doing at the end of day six, when God finished creating and entered into His rest.

> ❓ Read Gen. 2:1-3, 15; 3:8. Paint a picture of life in Gan Eden, with man dwelling in the Presence of the LORD. In what ways does the mishkan call man to Shabbat rest, without work, and with the LORD's Presence and protection?

Spirit-Filled Glory!

> **❝** *For the cloud of* ADONAI *was above the tabernacle during the day, and fire was in [the cloud] at night, so that all the house of Isra'el could see it throughout all their travels.* **❞** —*Exodus 40:38*

Immediately, the cloud covers the tent of meeting and the k'vod ADONAI (*glory of the LORD*) fills the mishkan (*dwelling*). God approves the completed work of Yisra'el by coming to dwell in the midst of His people!

> *With the work completed, God's sends His glory to fill His dwelling.*

What started as a people in slavery to an earthly kingdom is now elevated to a people at work for a divine king who leads them to the Land of their fathers.

Recall that in the week leading up to Shavuot, the cloud covers the mountain for six days. On Shavuot (day 50 after the Passover), God calls Moshe to where His glory dwelt on the summit of Mount Sinai (Ex. 24:15-16).

Here, Moshe waits. The call will come soon! VAYIKRA (*And He called*) to Moshe from the tent of meeting (Lev. 1:1). For now, Moshe is "unable to enter the tent of meeting" (Ex. 40:35), because of the tremendous intensity of the glory of God. As at Sinai on Shavuot, Moshe must wait to be called.

? *Read Luke 24:49-51. The followers of Yeshua are told to wait to be "equipped with power from above" (Lk. 24:49). Explain why Yeshua ascends to heaven, and why fire falls on believers awaiting God's glory on Shavuot.*

Déjà Vu   *Meander*

" And there I have made a place for the ark containing the covenant of ADONAI, which he made with our ancestors when he brought them out of the land of Egypt. "
                                                    — 1 Kings 8:21

God's Spirit punctuates the dedication of the first temple with the same dynamic witnessed at the dedication of the mishkan.

The LORD fills the temple with His glory.

This time, the cloud fills the house, and the kohanim (*priests*) cannot stand to minister the service (1 Ki. 8:10-11). Then, the k'vod ADONAI (*glory of the LORD*) fills the house of the LORD. This spectacular event is witnessed by all the people.

Next, Shlomo (*Solomon*) thanks the LORD for fulfilling His word that David's son would build a house and sit upon the throne (1 Ki. 8:20).

The concluding verse makes the interesting comment that Shlomo has "made a place for the ark containing the covenant of ADONAI" (1 KI. 8:21). Long ago, Moshe once spread the curtains to make the tent, and then followed up by bringing the ark with the tablets into the Holy of Holies (Ex. 40:17, 19, cf. Ex. 26:33). Now Shlomo walks the same walk, with the same result!

Read Jn. 14:2-3, 23. *Ultimately, the* LORD *Himself builds the house, but it is within the sanctuary of the human heart. What place does Yeshua prepare for His priests? What home does He make in the midst of believers?*

> **"** *because I will be merciful toward their wicked-nesses ..." By using the term, "new," he has made the first covenant "old"... on its way to vanishing altogether.* **"**
> —Hebrews 8:12a, 13

Labeling the covenant as "old" has led some to label Judaism as anachronistic. Actually, the content and aims of the "new" covenant have not changed!

> **The "new" covenant is designed to work with the same "old" people.**

The "new" covenant is still made with the House of Yisra'el, not the church (Heb. 8:8, 10); and its goal is still, "I will be their God, and they will be my people" (Heb. 8:10; Ex. 6:7). The first covenant had faults, because the people failed to stay wholehearted in relating to God and God responded by withdrawing His Presence (Heb. 8:7-9).

The "crowning affirma-tion" of the B'rit Chadashah (Heb. 8:1) is Messiah's entry into heaven as our Kohen Gadol. His entry provides believers with unlimited access to God's holy Presence! To grant access, God says, "I will be merciful toward their wickednesses and remember their sins no more" (Heb. 8:12). He helps overcome weakness in the flesh of those being sanctified.

> *Read Hebrews 8:12, Mt. 16:22. Peter said, "Heaven be merciful" when he hears that Yeshua must die. For this plea, Yeshua calls him Satan! How does Peter's plea for mercy contrast with God's mercy to believers' "wickedness?"*

Talk Your Walk . . .

Accountability takes center stage. No leader, not even the most elevated, is above accountability. In his humility, Moshe recognizes the principle of accountability and orders the audit. The report, given by Itamar, reads like a legal record from the archives. In today's language, P'KUDEI (*accountings of*) the materials used in the construction of the mishkan resembles an accounting firm's formal audit.

Construction activity spotlights the priestly vestments next. Exacting details describe how gold is brocaded with three different woolen materials and fine linen. The same materials woven into the curtains, a resting place for the Presence of the LORD, are also woven into the special vestments worn by the Kohen Gadol (*High Priest*). The Kohen Gadol is elevated to enter the Most Holy Place and walk past the k'ruvim (*cherubim*) into the visible Presence of God.

From the first day after Yom Kippur until the first day of Nisan, the people work hard to finish the work of making the mishkan (*dwelling*). Then, in seven acts, Moshe erects the mishkan

> *The work is completed, and God comes to dwell with His people.*

and positions its furniture—starting with placing God's Words on stone tablets in the ark in the throne room. With the work completed, God's glory surges into the mishkan with a light so intense that Moshe cannot enter to minister!

Oasis

. . . Walk Your Talk

D
o you believe that seeing God's visible Presence would inspire you to live differently? Thomas the doubter called the risen Yeshua, "My Lord and my God!" Yeshua answered him, "Have you trusted because you have seen me? How blessed are those who do not see, but trust anyway!" (Jn. 20:29). You fool yourself if you think that seeing God will change your behaviors. You must prepare to see God first! "How blessed are the pure in heart! for they will see God" (Mt. 5:8).

To prepare, spend time being transformed. Is your heart so pure that you act without an agenda? You must reserve the highest quality of time for abiding in the Presence of God. During this time, you will certainly be transformed. But your honest motivation must be only to please God!

The rest will take care of itself. You will change. Your tastes will change. The things that bring joy to your heart will change. Your greatest delight will bring joy to the LORD. Nothing will delight you more, because your tastes

> *Beyond transformation is the pure, holy desire to bring joy to the LORD.*

will have changed. And then, transformed, you will be granted the desires of your heart!

Shabbat Shalom!

Journey's

Sefer SH'MOT continues the progression of God's work to redeem man. God has raised up a royal family to become a nation to reach the nations of the world. This royal family now inherits the blessings conferred upon Adam and Noach, patriarchs of mankind. Noach's family had spread out, and seventy sons became seventy nations with seventy languages. In contrast, the sons of Yisra'el now unite and begin to reverse the movement of exile from Gan Eden.

The seventy sons journey to Egypt to unite. Their very blessing, to multiply exceedingly, leads to enslavement and a cry for redemption. God answers Yisra'el's cry for help. With a mighty hand, the LORD reveals Himself to His children and to the nations of the world.

God's fulfills a promise and redeems a nation.

With signs and wonders, He redeems Yisra'el from the grueling work of slavery. God elevates the nation as a holy priesthood, to live in close proximity to Him and to serve with gratitude in His dwelling.

On the way to nationhood, individuals are elevated to the redeemed work of holy service in the judiciary, in the priesthood, and in the army. Harrowing moments of disobedience occur, but Moshe intercedes for God to personally guide the nation. In the end, the nation obeys God down to the most minute of details. Heartfelt offerings are taken, the Dwelling is built, and then God's glory floods the heart of the nation!

End

In Judaism, redemption means freedom from bondage and long life in the Land of Promise. In Christianity, redemption means freedom from sin and the gift of eternal life. One conception is earth-centered, a ransom from bondage with freedom and justice for all; the other conception is heaven-centered, a ransom from death and the free gift of eternal life.

As we retell the story of the Exodus to our children, we recall God's work of redemption in freeing our nation from oppression to a foreign power. Our avodah (*work*) is elevated from agonizing slavery to worshipful *service*, freely given as t'rumah, a heartfelt *offering* lifted up to the Lord! This transformation of work into service puts exiled mankind on a spiritual path pointing back to Eden, an idyllic life in a world that's free from the consequences of the Fall.

Do you believe God can transform your life today? Are you ready to walk in God's highest dreams for your life? Are you willing to serve God freely, not enslaved by passions or unclean desires? Study, meditate, reflect, and feed on the scriptures. Let God's

> *Let God's Word redeem and transform your life.*

Word dwell in you, come alive in you, and take on a life of its own within you. Let His Word redeem and transform your life. Chazak, chazak, v'nit'chazek (*be strong, be strong, and may we be strengthened*) !!!

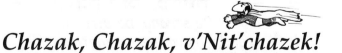

Chazak, Chazak, v'Nit'chazek!

Well, that's the end
of the Exodus story.
You can rest on your journey
and worship God's glory!
Then the beat goes on—
let the Torah roll
through Leviticus, Numbers,
and the rest of the scroll.
At the end of each book,
we take a break.
Chazak, Chazak, v'Nit'chazek!

חֲזַק חֲזַק וְנִתְחַזֵּק
Be strong, be strong,
and may we be strengthened!!!

Glossary

Ach'**av** (*Ahab*)

A**chaz** (*Ahaz*)

A**dam** (*Adam/humankind*)

ADONAI (*The LORD/* יהוה)

ADONAI-Tzva'**ot** (*the LORD of Hosts*)

Aha**ron** (*Aaron*)

al**eh** el**ai** (*ascend to Me!*)

A**lei**nu (*upon us/it is our duty, part of the liturgy*)

am s'**gulah** (*treasured people*)

Ano**chi** ADONAI Elo**hei**cha (*I Am the LORD, your God*)

an**shei**-cha**yil** (*men capable*)

A**ron** haE**dut** (*the Ark of the Testimony*)

a**rov** (*mixture*)

A**seret** haDi**brot** (*the Ten Words/Utterances/Commandments*)

a**sham** (*guilt offerings*)

A**vihu** (*Abihu*)

avo**dah** (*work, service*)

Av**ram** (*exalted father*)

Avra**ham** (*Abraham/father of a mass of nations*)

'**Aza** (*Gaza*)

Ba'**al** Ts'**fon** (*Baal Zephon, lit. Lord of the North*)

Ba-**cho**desh ha-shli**shi** (*in the third month*)

BaMIDBAR (*in the wilderness/ Book of Numbers*)

ba-mid**bar** (*into the wilderness*)

bat **kol** (*voice of the LORD*)

BCE (Before the Common Era)

b'**chol** m'la'**chah** (*in all creative activity*)

Beit-**El** (*Bethel*)

ben Tav'**el** (*the son of Tabeel*)

bimah (*high place*)

b'ha'**alot** Aha**ron** (*Aaron causes to go up*)

Bo (*enter!*)

B'REISHEET (*in the beginning/ Book of Genesis*)

B'**rit** Chada**shah** (*New Covenant/New Testament*)

b'**rit** o**lam** (*everlasting covenant*)

b'**sefer** (*into a book*)

B'SHALACH (*when he let go*)

B'SHALACH Par'**oh** (*when Pharaoh let go*)

B'tsal'**el** (*Bezalel/Shadow of God*)

b'**yad** ra**mah** (*with an upraised hand*)

chag l'ADONAI (*festival to the* LORD)

cha**mas** (*lawlessness*)

cha**metz** (*leavening*)

chami**shi** (*fifth*)

Chanuk**kah** (*Feast of Dedication, Hanukkah*)

Cha**ran** (*Haran, crossroads*)

chata'**t** (*sin offering*)

CHAYEI SARAH (*the life of Sarah*)

Cha**zak**, cha**zak**, v'nit'cha**zek**! (*Be strong, be strong, & may we be strengthened!*)

chen (*favor*)

che**sed** (*covenant loyalty*)

Cho**rev** (*Horeb*, lit. *desert, desolation*)

cho**shen** (High Priest's *breastplate*)

cho**shev** (lit. *work of thought, skill; the finest woven craftsmanship*)

chu**kot** (*statutes*)

Chur (*Hur*)

C'**na**'an (*Canaan*)

da**yenu** (enough for us)

D'VARIM (*words/Book of Deuteronomy*)

Eilim (*Elim*, place of *terebinths*)

Ein muk**dam** oo-m'u**char** ba**Torah** (*There is no early or late in the Torah*)

Ei**tam** (*Etham*)

ekev (*as a result of*)

ekev a**sher** sh'**ma**ta b'koli (*as a result that you listened to My voice*)

El'**azar** (*Eleazer*)

el lib'**cha** (*to your very heart*)

elo**him** (*god, judge*)

Elo**him** (*God, the judge*)

e**phod** (High Priest's *apron*)

erev **rav** (*the great conglomeration, the mixed multitude*)

eshma' b'ko**lo** (*I should listen to His voice*)

et-ha-**de**rech yel**chu** vahh (*the way, they must walk in it*)

ets**ba** elo**him** (*finger of God*)

Etz haCha**yim** (*the Tree of Life*)

exodus (Greek for *the way out*)

Gan **Eden** (*the Garden of Eden*/Paradise)

Ger**shom** (*stranger there*)

ha-elo**him** (*the judges/God*)

Haf**tarah** (*conclusion*/a reading from the Prophets)

Har-haElo**him** (*the mountain of God*)

Har Sinai (*Mt. Sinai*)

ha-shamayim (*the waters above*)
Hevel (*Abel*)
hit'allalti b'Mitzrayim (*I made a mockery of Egypt*)
hotsi' ADONAI etchem mi-zeh (*brings out the LORD all of you from this*)
Im shamo'a tishm'u b'koli (*if you listen diligently to My voice*)
Itamar (*Ithamar*)
ka'asher diber ADONAI b'yad Moshe (*just as the LORD had said by the hand of Moshe*)
ka'asher tsivah ADONAI et Moshe (*exactly as the LORD commanded Moshe*)
kadesh li (*sanctify to Me)*
kapporet (*cover, ark cover*)
kaved (*heavy, glorify*)
Kayin (*Cain*)
k'chol asher tsivah . . . ken asu/asah (*according to all God commanded . . . thus they/he did*)
k'chol ka'asher tsivah ADONAI et-Moshe; ken asu b'nei yisra'el et-kol-ha'avodah (*according to all that the LORD commanded Moshe, thus the children of Yisra'el finished all the work*)
k'dushah (*holiness*)
kes-YAH (abbreviation for throne of the *Holy One*)

k'hilah (*community*)
ki b'chozek yad (*because with a strong hand*)
Ki im shamo'a tish'ma b'kolo (*For if you indeed listen to his voice*)
kikar (*talent*, perhaps 66 lbs.)
KI TISA (*when you elevate*)
Kodesh Kodashim (*Holy of Holies*)
kofer (*ransom, half-shekel payment*)
kohanim (*priests*)
Kohen Gadol (*High Priest*)
Kohen haGadol (*the High Priest*)
k'ruvim (*cherubim*)
k'toret (*incense*)
k'tubah (*marriage contract*)
k'vod ADONAI (*glory of the LORD*)
l'avdahh v'shamrahh (*to work it and watch over it*)
LECH L'CHA (*go forth, yourself!*)
lishmo'a b'kolo (*to obey His voice*)
lo t'kalel (*do not curse or honor lightly*)
Lo yada'ti et- יהוה (*I do not know the LORD*)
ma'aseh choshev (*woven design*)
maftir (*concluding*)
Mah-t'rivun imadi? Mah-t'nasun et-haShem? (*For what

GLOSSARY • 213

do you quarrel with me? For what do you test ADONAI?)

man (Egyptian for *gift* or *coming from the sky every day*)

Marah (place of *bitter* waters)

Mashiach (*Messiah*)

Massah (*Massah, Testing*)

mi-beit avadim (*from the house of work/bondage*)

Mi chamocha? (*Who is like You?*)

Midrash (*exposition, rabbinical commentary on the Bible*)

Midyan (*Midian*)

MIKETZ (*at the end of*)

mikdash (*holy place/sanctuary/ dwelling/tabernacle*)

mikveh (*ritual bath, baptism*)

m'il (*overcoat*, High Priest's *robe made of blue wool*)

minchah (*tribute offering*)

Miryam (*Miriam*)

mishkan (*tabernacle/God's dwelling*)

Mishnah (*teachings, the Oral Law compiled in 220 CE*)

MISHPATIM (*judgments, rulings*)

Mitzrayim (*Egypt*)

m'norah (menorah/candelabra)

moftim (*wonders*)

Moshe (*Moses*)

M'rivah (*Meribah, Quarreling*)

Na'aseh v'nishma (*we will do and we will listen/obey*)

Nadav (*Nadab*)

nasi (*leader*)

ner tamid (*eternal light*)

nifla'ot (*wonders*)

nigash Moshe (*Moses drew near*)

NOACH (*Noah/ rest*)

nora (*awesome*)

N'vat (Nebat)

ohel moed (*tent of meeting*)

Oholi'av (*Oholiab, Tent of the Father*)

olah (*ascent offering, burnt or whole offering, holocaust*)

olat tamid (*daily/regular ascent offering*)

olot (plural for olah)

omer (5.1 pints)

otot (*signs*)

pachim (*thin leaves*)

Pakod pakad'ti (*I have watched over you/accounted for your account*)

parashah (Torah *portion*)

parashiot (Torah *portions*)

parochet (*partition, veil*)

Par'oh (*Pharaoh*)

p'dut (*redemption*)

pen yinachem (*lest they repent*)

pidyon ha-ben (*redemption of the son*)

Pi haChirot (*Pi-hahiroth, Mouth of Freedom*)

P'KUDEI (*accountings of*)

Ra'amses (*Rameses*)

rachamim (*compassion*)
R'fidim (*Rephidim*)
rishon (*first*)
Rivkah (*Rebecca*)
rokem (*a loose braiding*)
Ruach haKodesh (*Holy Spirit*)
r'vi'i (*fourth*)
Sar Shalom (*Prince of Peace*)
Sefer B'REISHEET (*Book of
    Genesis/in the beginning*)
Sefer haB'rit (*The Book of the
    Covenant*)
Sefer SH'MOT (*Book of Exodus/
    names*)
s'gulah (*treasure*)
Shabbat (*Sabbath*)
Shalach ami v'ya'avduni (*Let
    My people go that they may
    serve Me*)
Shalach et ami v'ya'avduni
    (*Let My people go that they
    may serve Me*)
shalem (*whole*)
sham'u l'kolecha (*listen to your
    voice*)
Sh'ar Yashuv (*A Remnant Will
    Return*)
Shavuot (*Feast of Weeks,
    Pentecost*)
Sh'chinah (*Presence*)
shem (*name*)
shemen zayit zach katit (*oil of
    olive, pure, pressed*)
shen v'ayin (*tooth and eye*)
sheni (*second*)

Shet (*Seth/appointed*)
Shirat haYam (*Song of the Sea*)
shishi (*sixth*)
sh'lamim (fellowship or *peace*
    offerings)
shlishi (*third*)
Shlomo (*Solomon*)
Shlomo haMelech (*King
    Solomon*)
Sh'ma b'koli (*Listen to my
    voice!*)
Sh'ma b'kolo (*Listen to His
    voice!*)
sh'mata b'kolo (*you listen to
    His voice*)
SH'MOT (*names*)
shvi'i (*seventh*)
sofeet (*final, as in the special
    forms for Hebrew letters chaf,
    mem, nun, fay, and tsadee*)
s'rafim (*guardian angels*)
Sukkot (*Succoth*)
tachashim (*dolphin/sea cow*)
Tanakh (תנ״ך, *an acronym for
    the Hebrew canon; Torah,
    Nevi'im/Prophets, and
    K'tuvim/Writings*)
tei'aseh (*she shall be made*)
t'fillin (*prayer boxes*)
t'horah (*purity*)
tikvah (*hope*)
Tishm'u b'koli (*listen to My
    voice*)
Tishm'u elav (*listen to Him*)
todah (*thank offerings*)

TOL'DOT (*generations*)

Torah (*instruction*/Pentateuch, Gen.-Dt.)

T'RUMAH (*offering, elevated to a higher level*)

t'rumot (plural of t'rumah)

ts'dakah (*charitable contributions*)

Tsidkiyahu (*Zedekiah*)

Tsiporah (*Zipporah*)

tsits (High Priest's *gold headplate*)

Tsiyon (*Zion*)

T'TSAVEH (*you shall command*)

Urim and Tumim (*lightings and perfections*, devices under High Priest's breastplate used for receiving prophetic direction)

v' (the conjunction *and*)

VA'ERA (*and I appeared*)

v'atem ta'harishun (*and you be still*)"

v'avadata et ha'avodah ha-zot (*you shall serve this service*)

VAYAKHEL (*and he assembled*)

Va-yar Yisra'el et-ha-yad ha-g'dolah (*and Israel saw the great hand*)

vaY'CHI (*and Jacob lived*)

vaYERA יהוה / ADONAI (*and the LORD appeared*)

vaYESHEV Ya'akov (*and Jacob settled*)

vaYETSE Ya'akov (*and Jacob went out*)

Va-yichad Yitro (*and Jethro prickled*)

VAYIGASH Y'hudah (*and Judah drew near*)

vayikahel (*assembled to demand*)

VAYIKRA (*and He called/Book of Leviticus*)

VAYISHLACH (*and he sent*)

Va-y'shalach Moshe et-chot'no (*And Moshe lets go of his father-in-law*)

V'chol ha'am ro'im et ha-kolot (*and all the people seeing voices/ thunder*)

V'eleh ha-mishpatim asher tasim lifneihem (*And these are the rulings you are to set before them*)

V'eleh SH'MOT (*and these are the names*)

v'hinei Mitzrayim nosea (*and behold Egypt marches*)

vidui (*confession*)

v'ikavdah (*and I will be glorified*)

v'ikavdah b'far'oh oov'chol-cheylo (*I will be glorified over Pharaoh and all his army*)

V'lo nacham Elohim (*But God did not lead*)

v'Sham'ru (*and you shall keep*, Ex. 31:16-17, part of the Shabbat liturgy) v'**sim** b'az**nei** Y'ho**shu**a (*and put into the ears of Joshua*)

v'tsiv'**cha** Elo**him** (*and God command you so!*)

v'yi**rash** zar'**acha** et-sha'ar o'y'**vav** . . . **e**kev a**sher** sh'-**ma**'ta b'**ko**li (*your seed will inherit the gates of his enemies . . . as a result that you listened to My voice*)

Ya'a**kov** (*Jacob*)

yak**ti**renah (*he causes to send up in smoke*)

Yam **Suf** (*Sea of Reeds*)

Yarov'**am** (*Jeroboam*)

Yechezk'**el** (*Ezekiel*)

Ye**shu**a (*Jesus/salvation*)

Ye**shu**a haMa**shi**ach (*Jesus the Messiah*)

Y'ho**shu**a (*Joshua*)

Y'hu**dah** (*Judah*)

Yirm'**ya**hu (*Jeremiah*)

Yisra'**el** (*Israel*)

YI**TRO** (*Jethro/abundance*)

Y'ru**sha**la**y**im (*Jerusalem*)

Y'sha'**ya**hu (*Isaiah*)

Yud-Heh-Vav-Heh יהוה (*the LORD, ADONAI*)

ze**k**her-Ama**lek** (a word-play doubling for *males of Amalek* and *memory of Amalek*)

ze**v**ach-pe**s**ach (*Passover festal sacrifice*)

zika**ron** (*memorial, reminder*)

ziv**chei** sh'la**mim** (*completion offerings*)

z'va**chim** (*offerings*)

z'va**chim** v'o**lot** (*festal sacrifices and ascent offerings*)

Bibliography

Alter, Robert. *The Art of Biblical Narrative.* Berkeley, CA: Basic Books, 1981.

Alter, Robert. *Genesis: Translation and Commentary.* First edition. New York: W. W. Norton & Company, 1996.

Attridge, Harold W. *The Epistle to the Hebrews.* In Helmut Koester (Gen. Ed.), *Hermeneia.* Philadelphia: Fortress Press, 1989.

Aune, David E. *Word Biblical Commentary: Revelation.* Nashville: Thomas Nelson Publishers, 1998.

Bav. Kam., Bava Kamma, see Schorr, *Talmud Bavli.*

Ben Avraham, Rabbi Alexander, and Sharfman, Rabbi Benjamin (Eds.). *The Pentateuch and Rashi's Commentary.* Brooklyn, NY: S. S. & R. Publishing Company, Inc. (also Philadelphia: Press of the Jewish Publication Society), 1976.

Ber., Berachot, see Schorr, *Talmud Bavli.*

Blackman, Philip. *Mishnayoth.* Vols. 1-6. Second edition. Gateshead: Judaica Press, 1983.

Bodenheimer, F. S. "The Manna of Sinai," *Biblical Archaeologist,* 10, 1, (1947), pp. 2-6.

Bruce, F. F. *The New International Commentary on the New Testament: The Epistle to the Hebrews.* Grand Rapids, MI: Wm. B. Eerdmans Publishing Company, 1979.

Bullinger, E. W. *Figures of Speech Used in the Bible.* Grand Rapids, MI: Baker Book House, 1987. (Original work published in 1898).

Carson, D. A. *Showing the Spirit: A Theological Exposition of 1 Corinthians 12-14.* Grand Rapids: Baker Book House, 1987.

Cassuto, U. *A Commentary on the Book of EXODUS.* Transl. from Hebrew by Israel Abrahams. Jerusalem: The Magnes Press, 1997. (Original work published in 1951).

The CD Rom Judaic Classics Library. Chicago: Institute for Computers in Jewish Life & Davka Corporation, 1991-1995.

Childs, Brevard S. *Biblical Theology of the Old and New Testaments: Theological Reflection on the Christian Bible*. Minneapolis: Fortress Press, 1993.

Cohen, A. (Gen. Ed.). *Soncino Books of the Bible*. Volumes 1-14. London: The Soncino Press Limited, 1978.

Concordance to the Novum Testamentum Graece. Third edition. Berlin: Walter De Gruyter, 1987.

Delitzsch, see Keil and Delitzsch.

de Vaux, Roland. *Ancient Israel: Social Institutions*. Volume 1. New York: McGraw-Hill, 1965.

Drazin, Israel, Trans. *Targum Onkelos: An English Translation of the Text with Analysis and Commentary*. Based on the A. Sperber and A. Berliner Editions. Center for Judaic Studies, the University of Denver: Ktav Publishing House, 1990.

Driver, S. R., Plummer, A., and Briggs, C. A. (Gen. Eds.). *The International Critical Commentary on the Holy Scriptures of the Old and New Testaments*. Edinburgh: T. & T. Clark, 1979. (Original work published 1896-1924).

Durham, John I. *Word Biblical Commentary: Exodus*. Waco, TX: Word Books, Publishers, 1987.

Ellingworth, Paul. *The New International Greek New Testament Commentary: The Epistle to the Hebrews*. Grand Rapids, MI: William B. Eerdmans Publishing Company, 1993.

Elwell, W. A. (Ed.). *Evangelical Dictionary of Theology*. Grand Rapids, MI: Baker Book House, 1984.

Eruvin, see Schorr, *Talmud Bavli*.

Evans, Louis H., Jr. *The Communicator's Commentary: Hebrews*. Dallas: Word Publishing, 1985.

Even-Shoshan, Avraham (Ed.). *New Concordance for the Torah, Prophets, and Writings*. Jerusalem: Sivan Press, 1977.

Fee, Gordon D. *The New International Commentary on the New Testament: The First Epistle to the Corinthians*. Grand Rapids: Wm. B. Eerdmans Publishing Company, 1987.

Feinberg, Jeffrey Enoch. *Walk GENESIS!* Baltimore: Lederer/Messianic Jewish Communications, 1998.

Fox, Everett. *The Schocken Bible: The Five Books of Moses.* Volume I. Dallas: Word Publishing, 1995.

Frankel, Ellen and Teutsch, Betsy P. (1992). *The Encyclopedia of Jewish Symbols.* Northvale, NJ: Jason Aronson, 1992.

Friedman, Rabbi Alexander Zusia. *Wellsprings of Torah.* Transl. by Gertrude Hirschler. New York: Judaica Press, Inc., 1990.

Furnish, Victor P. *II Corinthians.* The Anchor Bible. NY: Doubleday, 1984.

Gellis, Maurice and Gribetz, Dennis. *The Glory of Torah Reading.* Monsey, NY: M.P. Press, Inc., 1996.

Ginzberg, Louis. *The Legends of the Jews.* Transl. by Paul Radin. Volume 3: *Bible Times and Characters from the Exodus to the Death of Moses.* Philadelphia: Jewish Publication Society, 1911.

Ginzberg, Louis. *The Legends of the Jews.* Volume 6: *Notes to Volumes 3 and 4, From Moses in the Wilderness to Esther.* Philadelphia: Jewish Publication Society, 1928.

Gittin, see Schorr, *Talmud Bavli.*

Hamilton, Victor P. *The New International Commentary on the Old Testament: The Book of Genesis.* Grand Rapids, MI: William B. Eerdmans Publishing Company, 1990.

Hareuveni, Nogah. *Nature in Our Biblical Heritage.* Kiryat Ono: Neot Kedumim, 1980.

Herczeg, Rabbi Yisrael Isser Zvi (Ed.). *The Torah: With Rashi's Commentary Translated, Annotated, and Elucidated: Shemos/Exodus.* Volume 2. Artscroll Series/The Sapirstein Edition. Brooklyn: Mesorah Publications, Ltd., 1995.

Hertz, Dr. J. H. (Ed.). *The Pentateuch and Haftorahs.* Second edition. London: Soncino Press, 1975.

Hirsch, Samson Raphael, Trans. *The Pentateuch, Haftarah, and the Five Megillot.* Ed. by Ephraim Oratz. New York: The Judaica Press, Inc., 1990. (English translation by Gertrude Hirschler; German work published in 1867-1878).

Holy Bible: Authorized King James Version. Nashville: Royal Publishers, Inc., 1971.

Hubbard, Robert L. "#3828 Yasha" in W. A. VanGemeren (Gen.

Ed.), *New International Dictionary of New Testament Theology and Exegesis* (Vol. 2, pp. 556-562). Grand Rapids, MI: Zondervan Publishing House, 1997.

Ibn Ezra, see Schorr, *Talmud Bavli.*

ibn Paquda, R. Bachya. *Duties of the Heart.* Transl. by Moses Hyamson. Jerusalem: Feldheim Publishers, 1986. (Translated from Arabic into Hebrew by R. Yehuda Ibn Tibbon).

JPS, Jewish Publication Society, see *Tanakh.*

Kahan, Rabbi Aharon. *The Taryag Mitzvos.* Brooklyn: Keser Torah Publications, 1988. (Based on the classical Sefer haChinuch).

Kantor, Mattis. *The Jewish Time Line Encyclopedia: A Year-by-Year History from Creation to the Present.* Northvale, NJ: Jason Aronson, Inc., 1989.

Kaplan, Rabbi Aryeh. *The Living Torah.* Brooklyn: Maznaim Publishing Corporation, 1981.

Keil, C. F. and Delitzsch, F. *Commentary on the Old Testament.* , Transl. by James Martin. Volumes 1-10. Grand Rapids, MI: William B. Eerdmans Publishing Company, 1976.

Kent, Homer A. *The Epistle to the Hebrews.* Grand Rapids, MI: Baker Book House, 1985.

Kidd., Kiddushin, see Schorr, *Talmud Bavli.*

Kiene, Paul F. *The Tabernacle of God in the Wilderness of Sinai.* Grand Rapids: Zondervan, 1977.

KJV, King James Version, see *Holy Bible.*

Kohlenberger, John R. III (Ed.). *The NIV Interlinear Hebrew-English Old Testament.* Grand Rapids, MI: Zondervan Publishing House, 1979.

Kolatch, Alfred J. *The Complete Dictionary of English and Hebrew First Names.* Middle Village, NY: Jonathan David Publishers, Inc., 1984.

Lachs, Samuel Tobias. *A Rabbinic Commentary on the New Testament.* Hoboken, NJ: Ktav Publishing House, Inc., 1987.

Lane, William L. *Hebrews: A Call to Commitment.* Peabody, MA: Hendrickson Publishers, 1988.

Lane, William L. *Word Biblical Commentary: Hebrews 1-13.* Volumes 47a, 47b. Waco, TX: Word Books, Publisher, 1991.

Leibowitz, Nehama. *New Studies in Shemot (Exodus).* Transl. by Aryeh Newman. Volumes 1-2. Jerusalem: The World Zionist Organization, 1981.

Lev. R., Leviticus Rabbah, see *The CD Rom Judaic Classics Library.*

Mare, W. Harold and Harris, Murray J. *The Expositor's Bible Commentary: 1 & 2 Corinthians.* Grand Rapids: Zondervan, 1995.

Mekhilta According to Rabbi Ishmael: An Analytical Translation. Transl. by Jacob Neusner. Volumes 1 & 2. Atlanta: Scholars Press, Brown Judaic Studies, 1988.

Mekhilta, Bachodesh, see *Mekhilta,* Vol. 2.

Mid. HaGadol, Midrash HaGadol, see *The CD Rom Judaic Classics Library.*

Milgrom, Jacob. *Studies in the Cultic Theology and Terminology.* Leiden, 1983.

Milgrom, Jacob. *Numbers* (JPS Commentary). Philadelphia, 1990.

Milgrom, Jacob. *Leviticus 1-16* (Anchor Bible, vol. 3). New York, 1991.

Mish. Kidd., Mishnah Kiddushin, see Blackman, *Mishnayoth.*

Mizrachi, Elijah, see Rashi, 1995.

Mounce, Robert H. *The International Commentary on the New Testament: The Book of Revelation.* Grand Rapids: Wm. B. Eerdmans, 1977.

Nachshoni, Yehuda. *Studies in the Weekly Parashah.* Transl. by Raphael Blumberg. Volume 2: Sh'mos. Brooklyn: Mesorah Publications, Ltd., 1988.

The New English Bible. Standard edition. New York: Oxford University Press, 1971.

Novum Testamentum Graece. Nestle-Aland Edition. Stuttgart: Deutsche Bibelstiftung, 1981.

Or HaChaim, Rabbi Chaim ben Attar, see Stone.

Pes., Pesachim, see Schorr, *Talmud Bavli.*

Plaut, W. Gunther. *The Haftarah Commentary.* Transl. by Chaim

Stern. New York: UAHC Press, 1996.

Radak, Rabbi David Kimchi, see Schorr, *Talmud Bavli*.

Ramban, Rabbi Moshe ben Nachman, also Nachmanides, see Schorr, *Talmud Bavli* or *Ramban: Commentary on the Torah*. Transl. by Rabbi Dr. Charles B. Chavel. New York: Shilo Publishing House, Inc., 1973.

Rashi, see Ben Avraham, Rabbi Abraham et al., 1976.

Rashi, see Herczek, Rabbi Yisrael Isser Zvi, 1995.

Rashi, Men., Menachot, see Schorr, *Talmud Bavli*.

Rienecker, Fritz. *A Linguistic Key to the Greek New Testament*. Transl. and revised by Cleon L. Rogers, Jr. Volumes 1-2. Grand Rapids: Zondervan Publishing House, 1976.

Robertson, A. T. *Word Pictures in the New Testament*. Grand Rapids, MI: Baker Book House, 1932.

Sailhamer, John H. *The Pentateuch as Narrative*. Grand Rapids, MI: Zondervan Publishing House, 1992.

Sanh., Sanhedrin, see Schorr, *Talmud Bavli*.

Scherman, Rabbi Nosson (Gen. Ed.). *The Chumash*. Ed. by Rabbi Hersh Goldwurn, Rabbi Avie Gold, and Rabbi Meir Zlotowitz. Artscroll Series, The Stone Edition. Brooklyn: Mesorah Publications, Ltd., 1995.

Schorr, Rabbi Yisroel Simcha (Gen. Ed.). *Talmud Bavli*. The Artscroll Series, Schottenstein Edition. Brooklyn: Mesorah Publications, Ltd., 1993.

Sforno, Ovadiah. *Commentary on the Torah*. Transl. by Rabbi Raphael Pelcovitz. The Artscroll Mesorah Series. Brooklyn: Mesorah Publications, Ltd., 1997.

Shabb., Shabbos, see Schorr, *Talmud Bavli*.

Shulman, Eliezer. *The Sequence of Events in the Old Testament*. Transl. by Sarah Lederhendler. Fifth edition. Jerusalem: Investment Co. of Bank Hapoalim and Ministry of Defense— Publishing House, 1987.

Sifre: A Tannaitic Commentary on the Book of Deuteronomy. Yale Judaica Series, 24. Transl. by Reuven Hammer. New Haven: Yale University Press, 1986.

Smalley, Stephen S. *Word Biblical Commentary: 1, 2, 3 John*. Volume 51. Dallas: Word Books, 1984.

Sot., Sotah, see Schorr, *Talmud Bavli*.

Stern, David H., Trans. *Jewish New Testament*. Clarksville, MD: Jewish New Testament Publications, 1991.

Stern, David H. *Jewish New Testament Commentary*. Clarksville, MD: Jewish New Testament Publications, 1992.

Sternberg, Meir. *The Poetics of Biblical Narrative*. Bloomington: Indiana University Press, 1987.

Stone Edition, see Scherman, Rabbi Nosson (Gen. Ed.).

Talmud [Zev. 54a], see Schorr, *Talmud Bavli*.

Tanakh, The Holy Scriptures: The New JPS Translation According to the Traditional Hebrew Text. Philadelphia: Jewish Publication Society, 1985.

Tanch., Tanchuma, see Schorr, *Talmud Bavli*.

Tikkun Kor'im haM'fuar. Brooklyn, NY: Im haSefer, 1994.

Webster's Seventh New Collegiate Dictionary. Springfield, MA: G. & C. Merriam Company, Publishers, 1963.

Werblowsky, Dr. R. J. Zwi and Wigoder, Dr. Geoffrey (Eds.). *The Encyclopedia of the Jewish Religion*. Jerusalem: Masada Press Ltd., 1967.

Wigoder, Geoffrey (Gen. Ed.). "Redemption," in *The Encyclopedia of Judaism*. NY: Macmillan Publishing Company, 1989.

Wigram, George V. *The Englishman's Hebrew and Chaldee Concordance of the Old Testament*. Grand Rapids, MI: Baker Book House, 1980. (Original work published in 1843).

Yoma, see Schorr, *Talmud Bavli*.

Zev., Zevachim, see Schorr, *Talmud Bavli*.